Mel Bay Presents

BEN MONDER COMPOSITIONS

BY BEN MONDER

Engraving by Jeremey Poparad

Cover Photograph by Bill Douthart

Back Photograph by Ralph Gibson

3 4 5 6 7 8 9 0

© 2008 BY MEL BAY PUBLICATIONS, INC., PACIFIC, MO 63069.
ALL RIGHTS RESERVED. INTERNATIONAL COPYRIGHT SECURED. B.M.I. MADE AND PRINTED IN U.S.A.
No part of this publication may be reproduced in whole or in part, or stored in a retrieval system, or transmitted in any form
or by any means, electronic, mechanical, photocopy, recording, or otherwise, without written permission of the publisher.

Visit us on the Web at www.melbay.com — E-mail us at email@melbay.com

Technical Guide to the Charts

Slurs indicate hammer-ons or pull-offs.

Brackets are used to indicate barres. Often a finger will be used to barre only 2 or 3 strings (mini-barres) - the length of the bracket will indicate this.

D.B. means "diagonal barre." This is done by putting the tip of the finger on the lower note(s) and the back part of the finger on the upper note(s).

Harmonics, **artificial** or **natural**, are indicated by a diamond shaped note.

Numbers next to the notes indicate **finger**, while numbers in circles above the notes indicate **string**.

L.H. means left hand, **R.H.** means right hand.

R.H.H.O. means "right-hand hammer-on." The finger to be used on the right hand will be given in these instances.

T means thumb (left hand)

In the few instances that I provide right hand fingerings I use classical notation: **p=thumb, i=index finger, m=middle finger, a=ring finger**.

3. Often when a chord is apeggiated I want the notes to ring out, but adding all the slurs necessary to notate this precisely would cause the chart to look quite confusing. Use your own judgement or refer to the recording for guidance.

If a passage is repeated in a tune, I usually won't give the fingering a second time.

Tempo markings are approximate.

Table of Contents

Dust 4	Oceana 133
Echolalia 15	O.K. Chorale 168
Ellenville 24	Orbits 170
Flux 51	Propane Dream 189
Gemini 62	Red Shifts 196
Hatchet Face 69	Rooms of Light 200
In Memoriam 97	Sleep 224
Luteous Pangolin .. 102	Spectre 229
Mistral 109	Sunny Manitoba 238
Muvseevum 126	Windowpane 240

Foreword

Compositional diversity is indicative of strong writing. This book presents some of the most heterogeneous music imaginable. The following pieces display experimentation with various harmonic, technical and textural possibilities of the guitar within solo, trio and quartet (guitar, bass, drums, voice) settings. The music, while rooted in jazz improvisation, represent Monder's experience in a variety of musical idioms - jazz, classical, rock, and beyond - reflecting a thorough survey of the music of our time.

The music in this book was culled from a 20 year period of writing, and the pieces can all be found on Monder's four recordings as a leader: Flux, Dust, Excavation, and Oceana. The collection does justice to Monder's depth as a composer, and was compiled with the student and fellow musician in mind; each piece was selected for the unique technical challenges it presents to the performer, including unusual fingerings, alternate tunings, and more.

This book is documentation of one of the leading composers of our time. The product in your hands will provide you with countless hours of challenges and stimulation - hopefully enjoyment, too! Personally, I can't wait to sink my teeth into it.

Collin Bay

May, 2008

Dust

Ben Monder

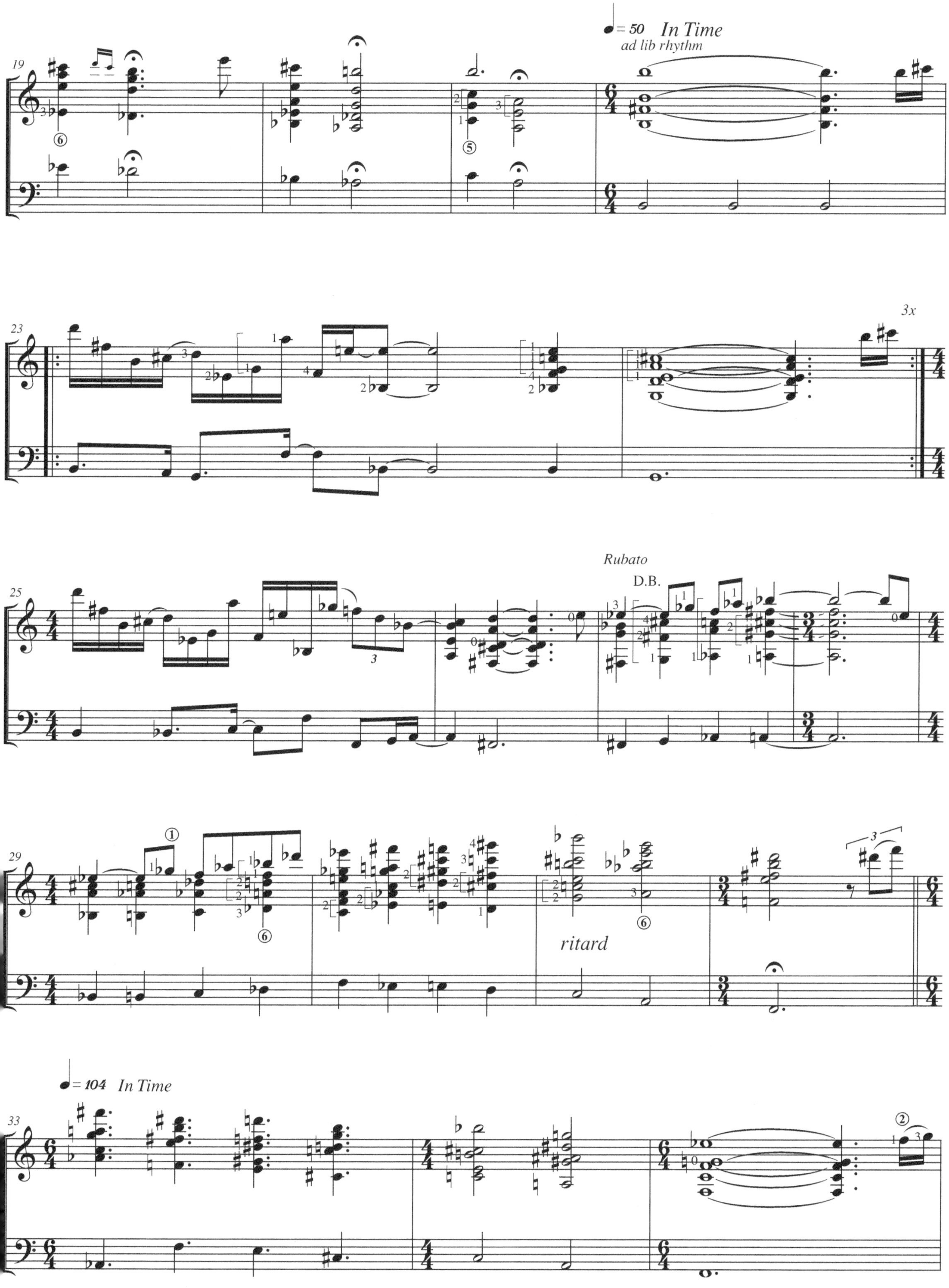
♩= 50 In Time
ad lib rhythm
3x
Rubato
D.B.
ritard
♩= 104 In Time

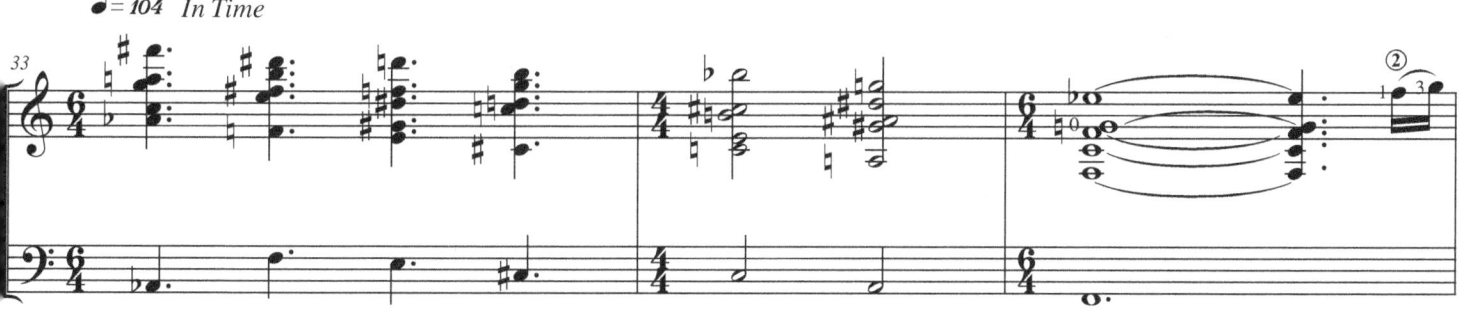

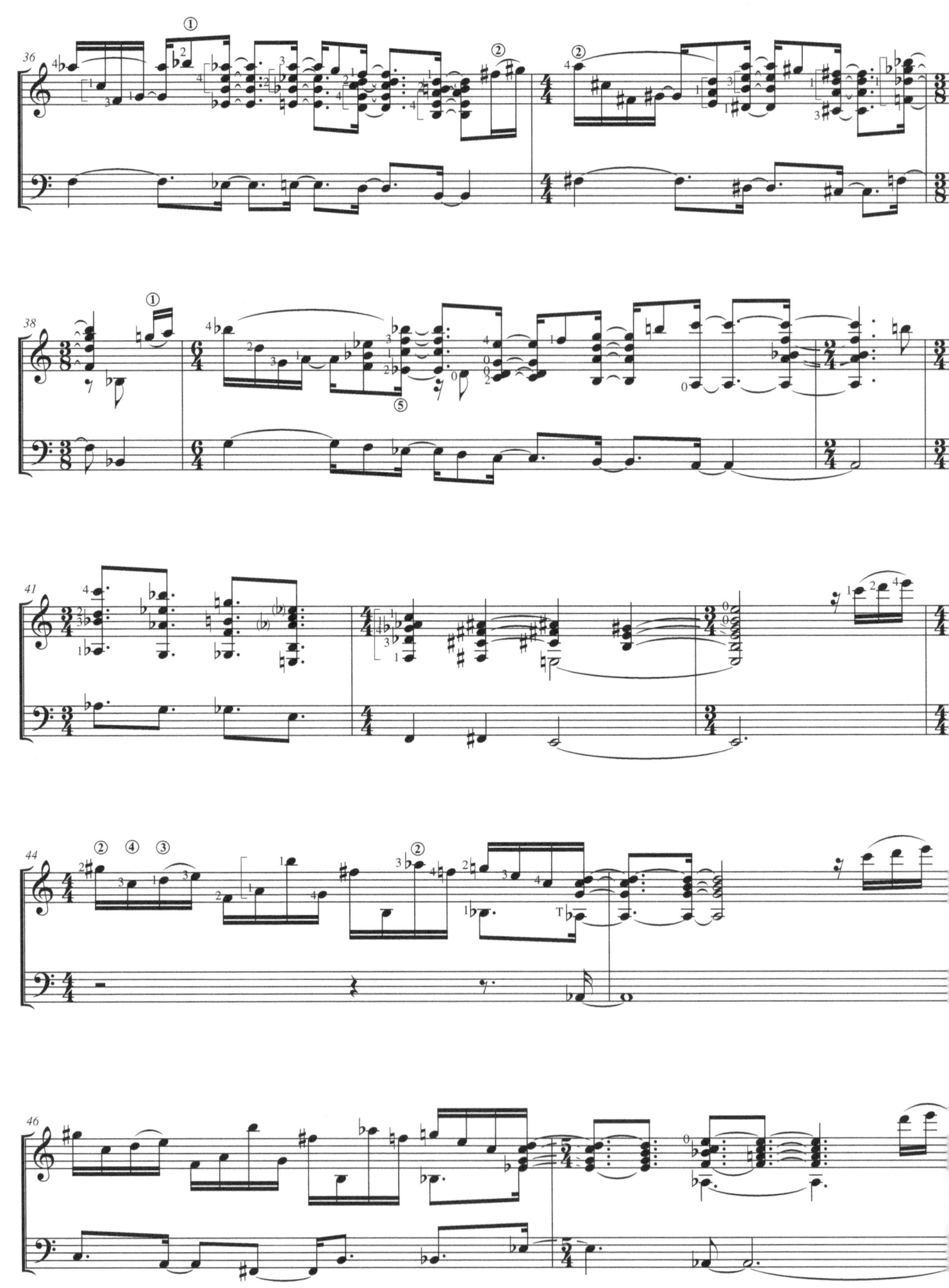

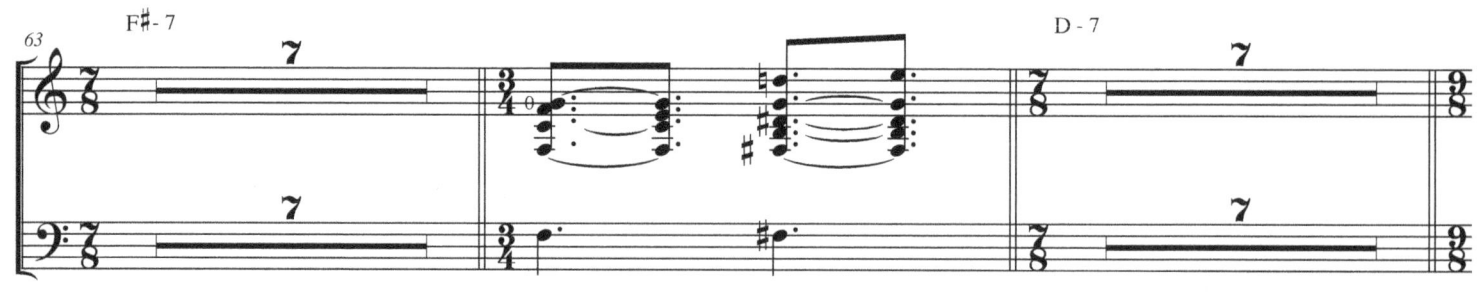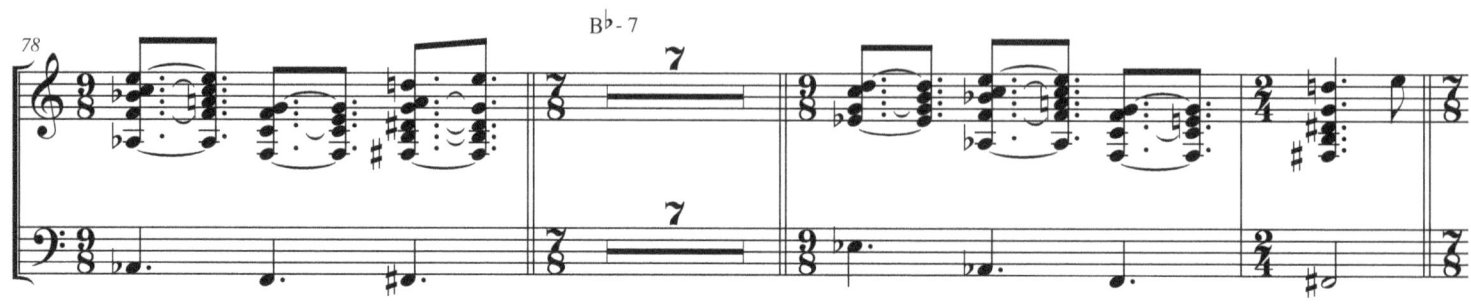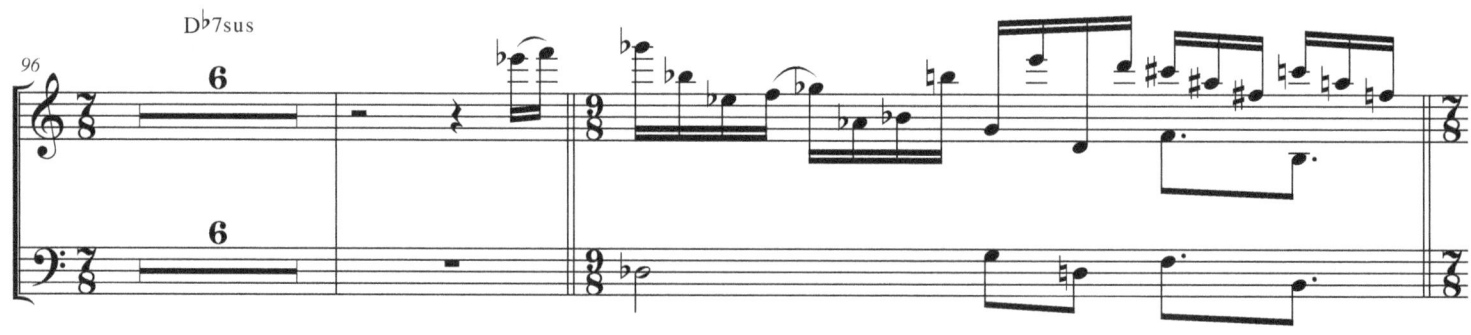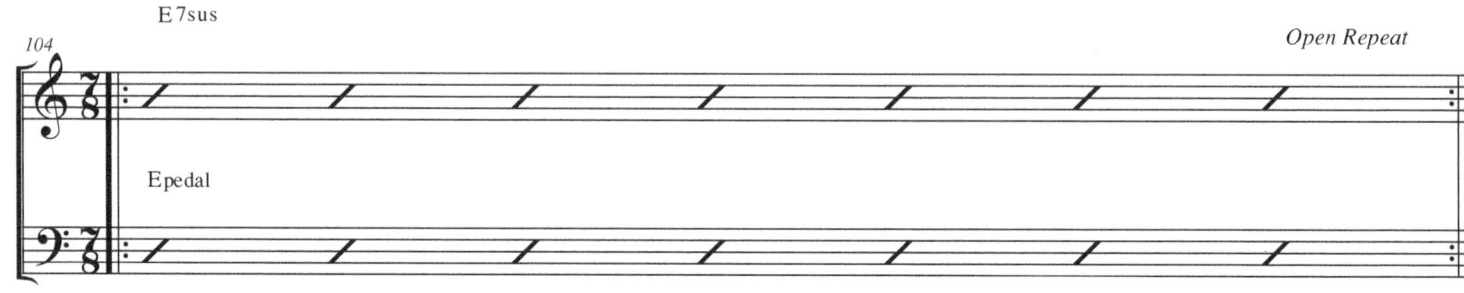

Echolalia

Ben Monder

Ellenville

Ben Monder

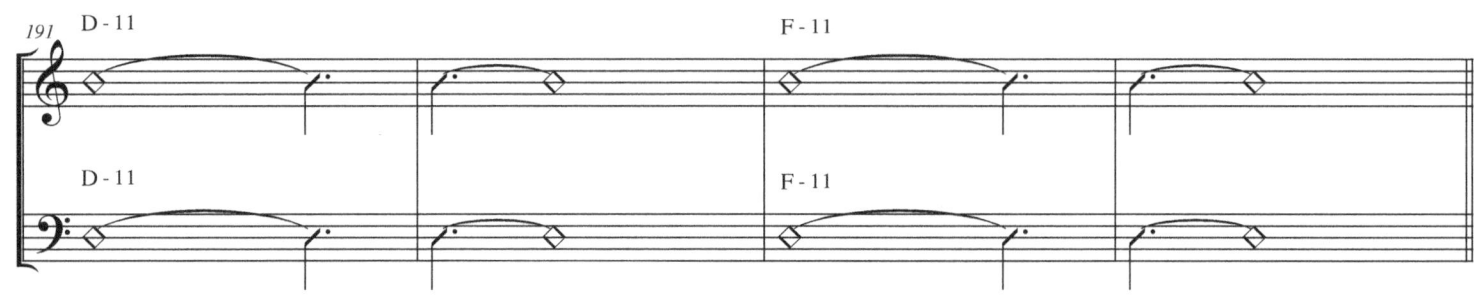
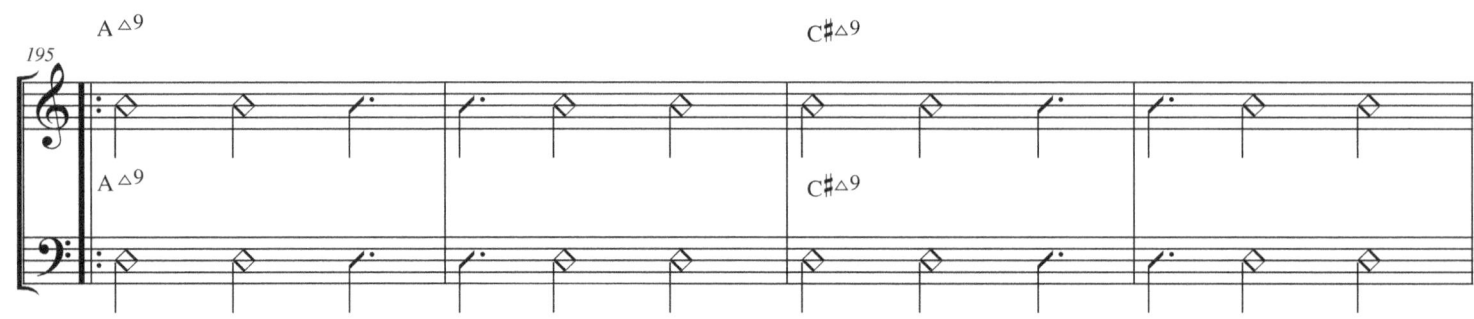
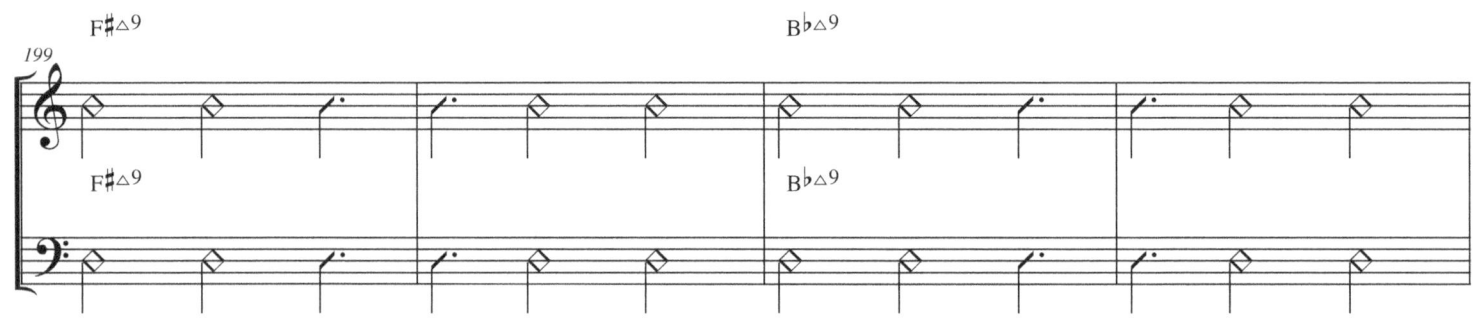
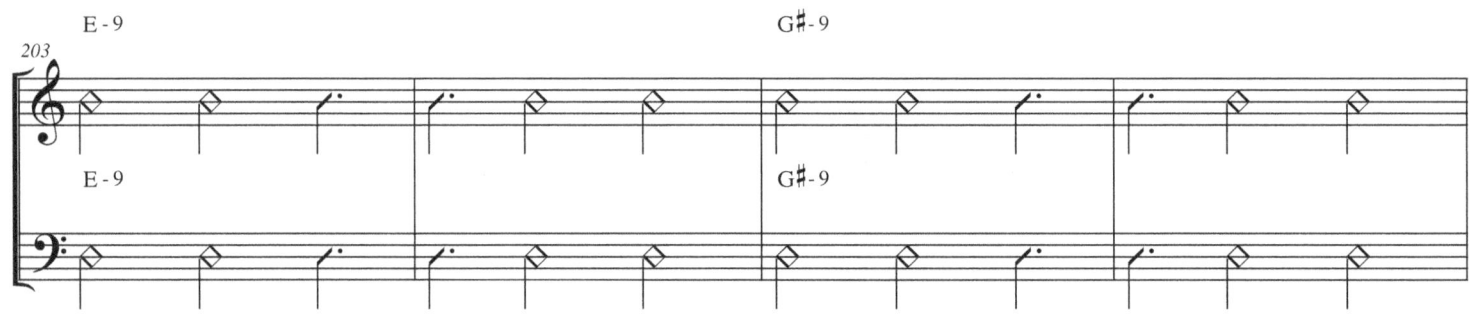
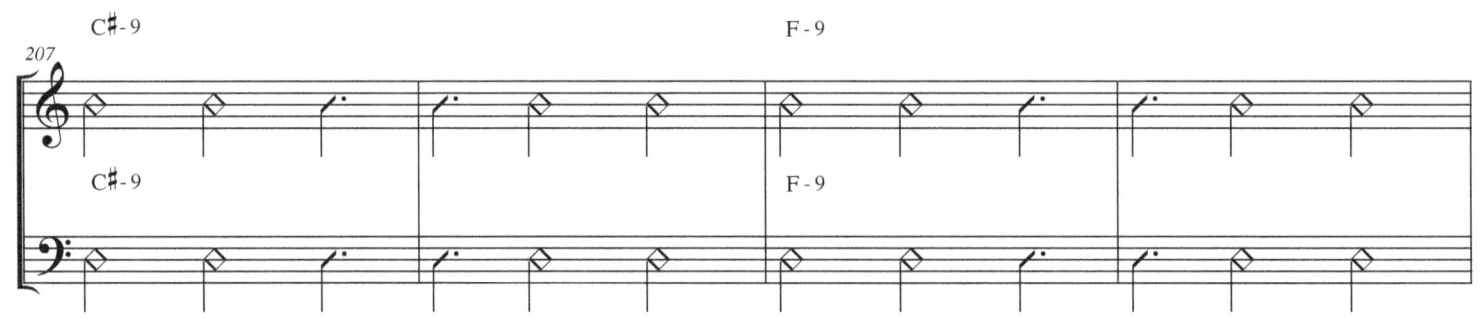

Flux

Ben Monder

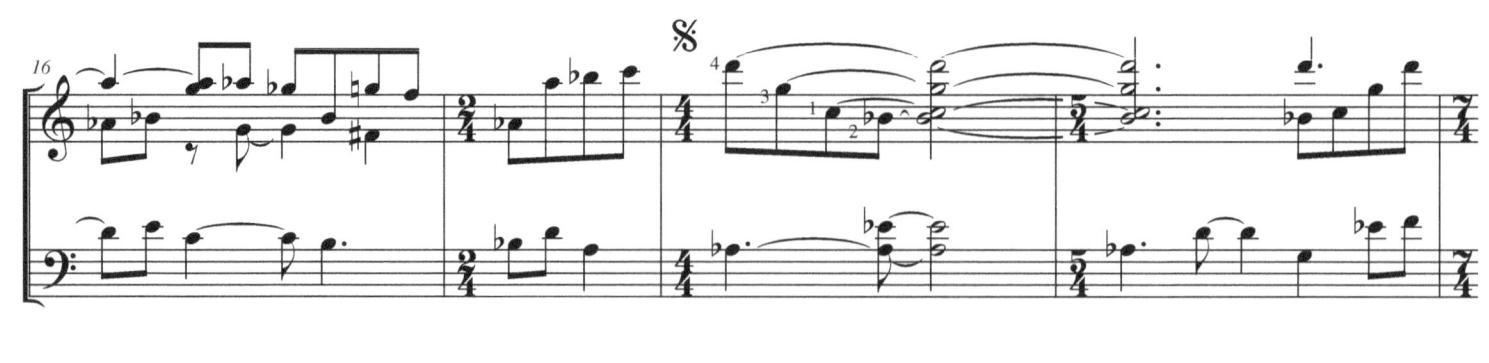

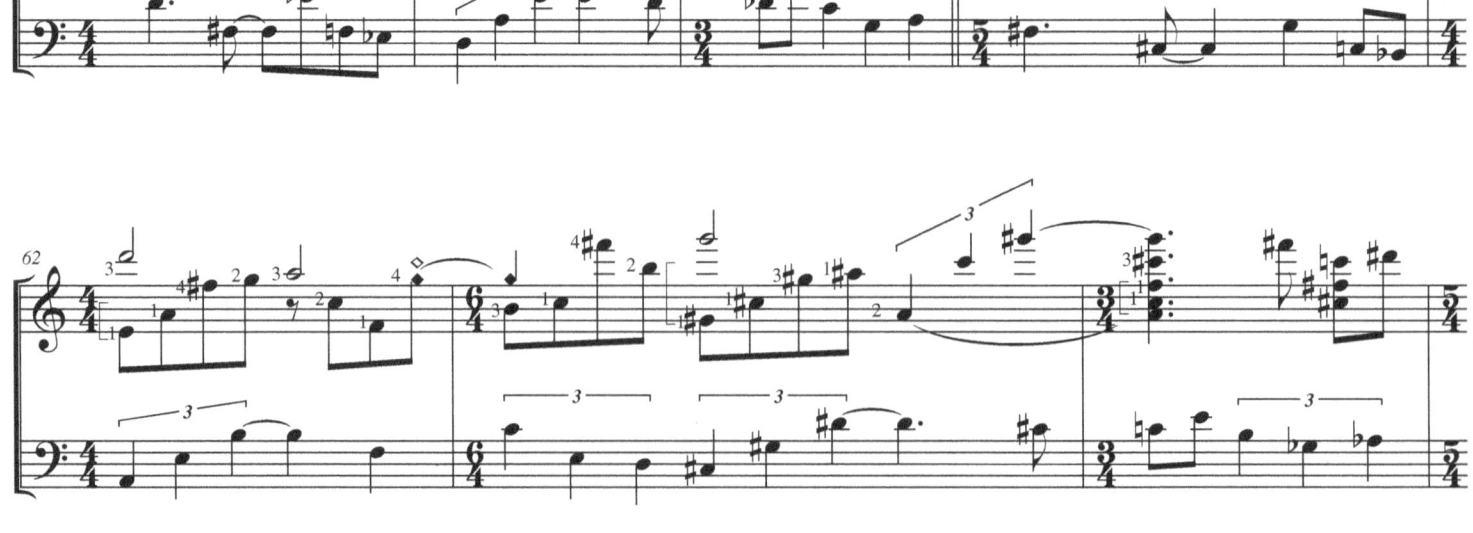

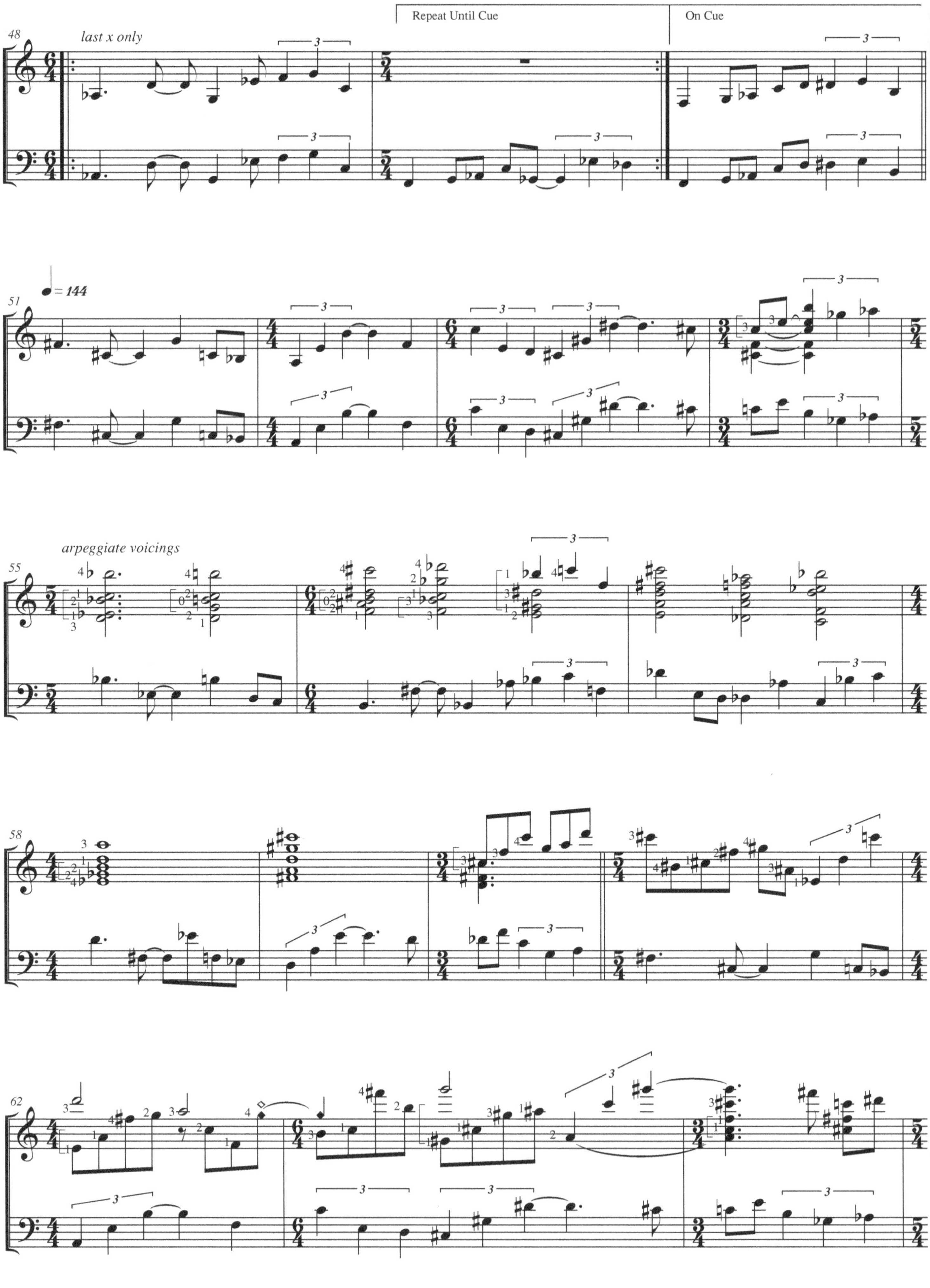
Repeat Until Cue
On Cue
48
last x only
51
= 144
55
arpeggiate voicings
58
62

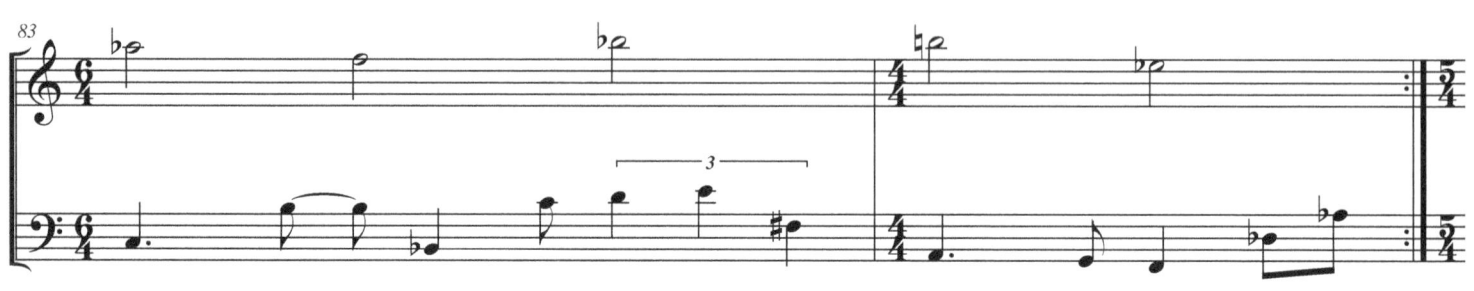

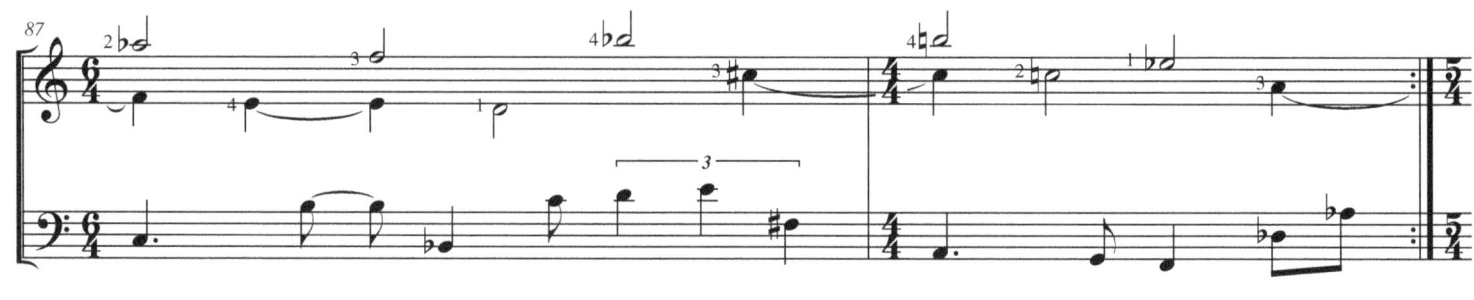

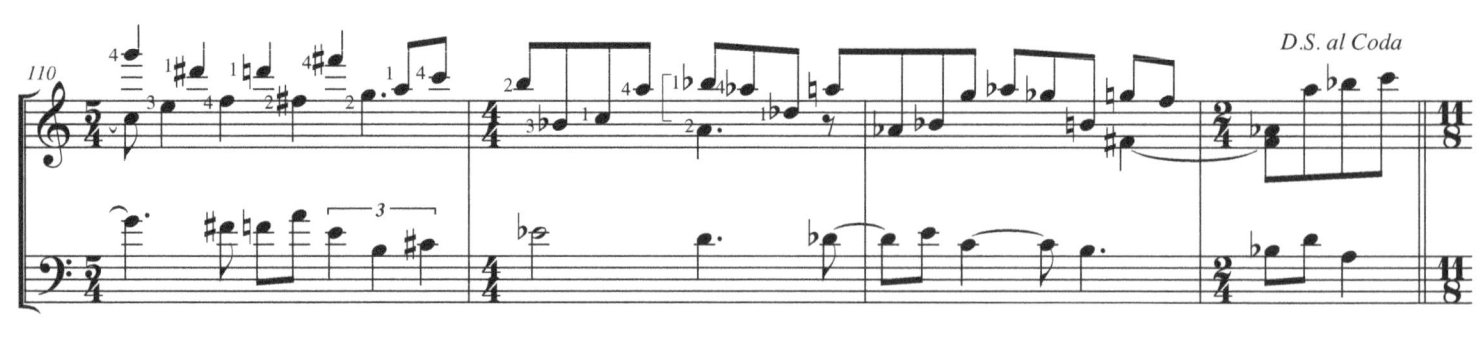
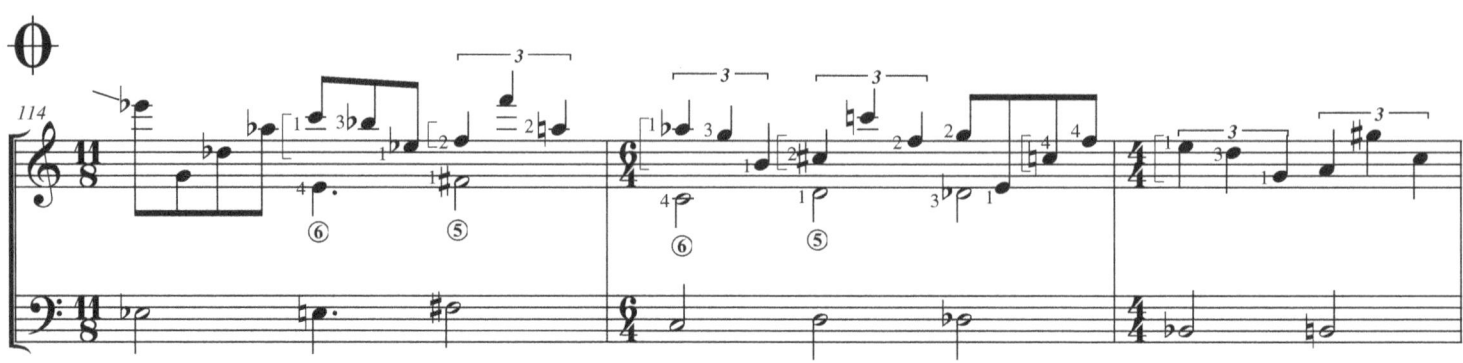

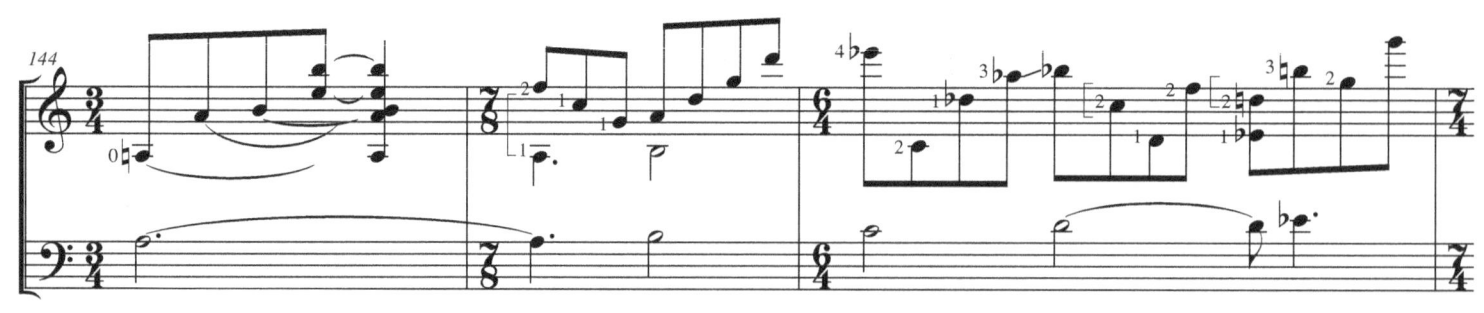

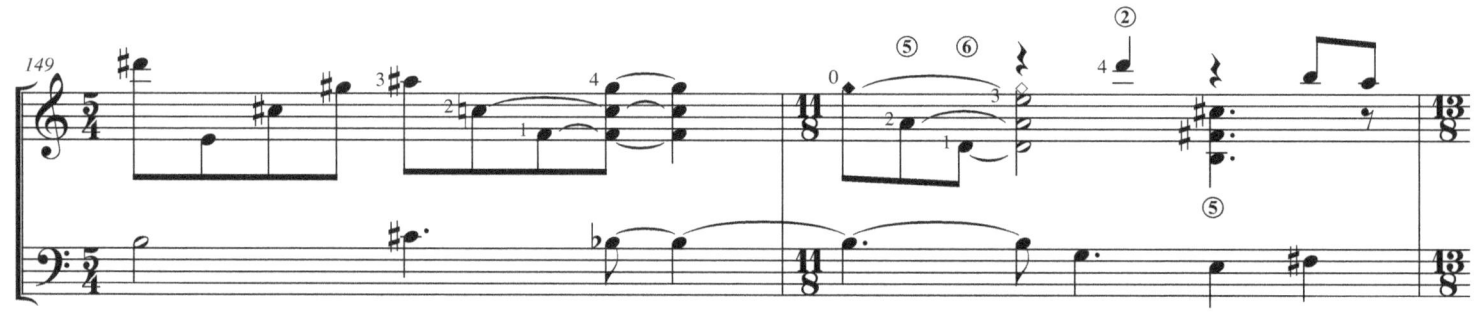
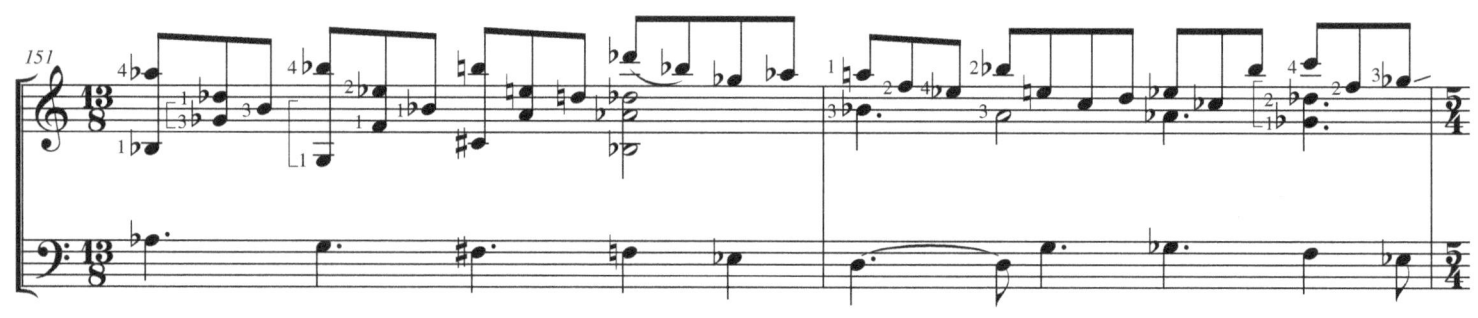
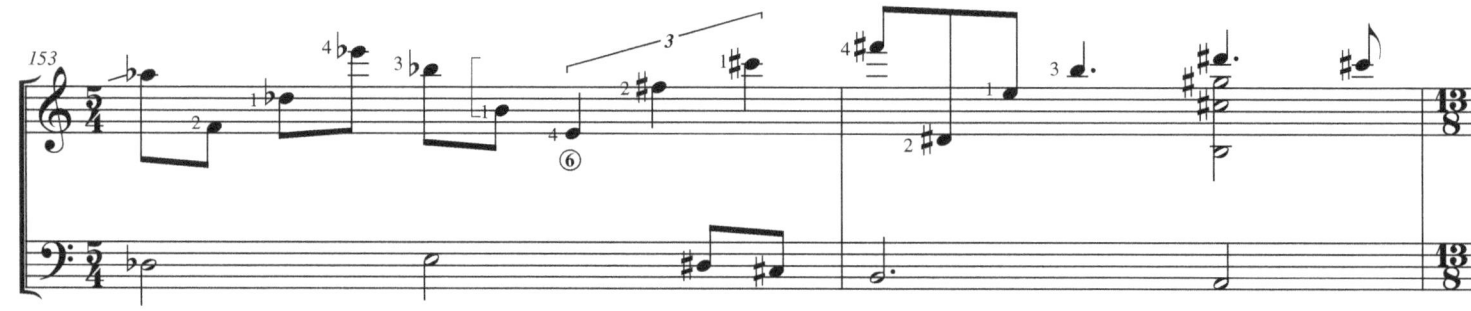

Gemini

Ben Monder

Continue bass solo, play as written last 2x

Hatchet Face

Ben Monder

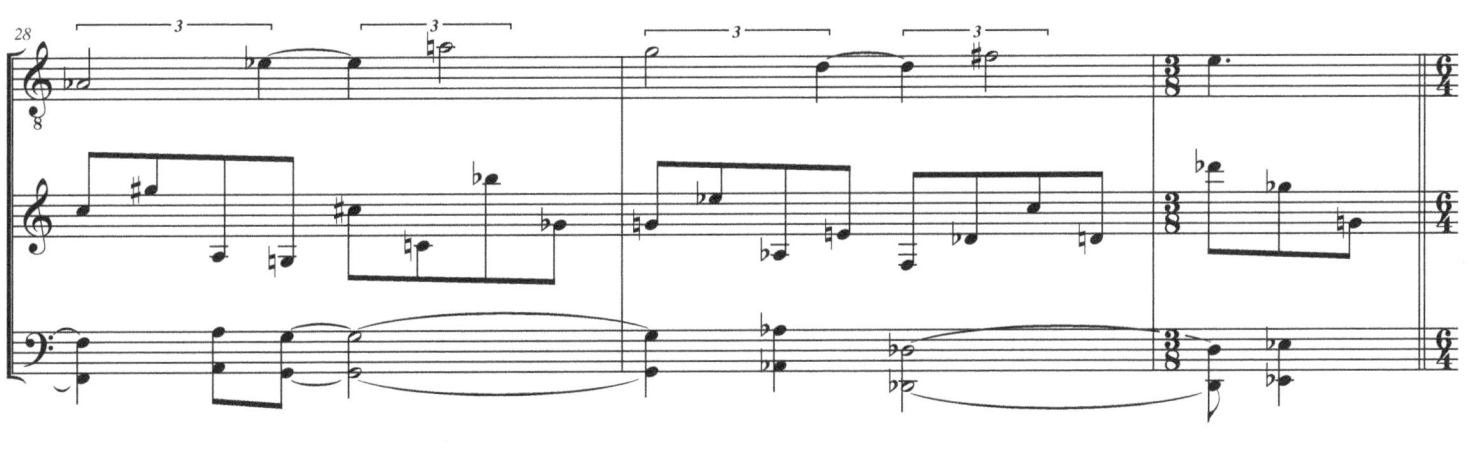

71

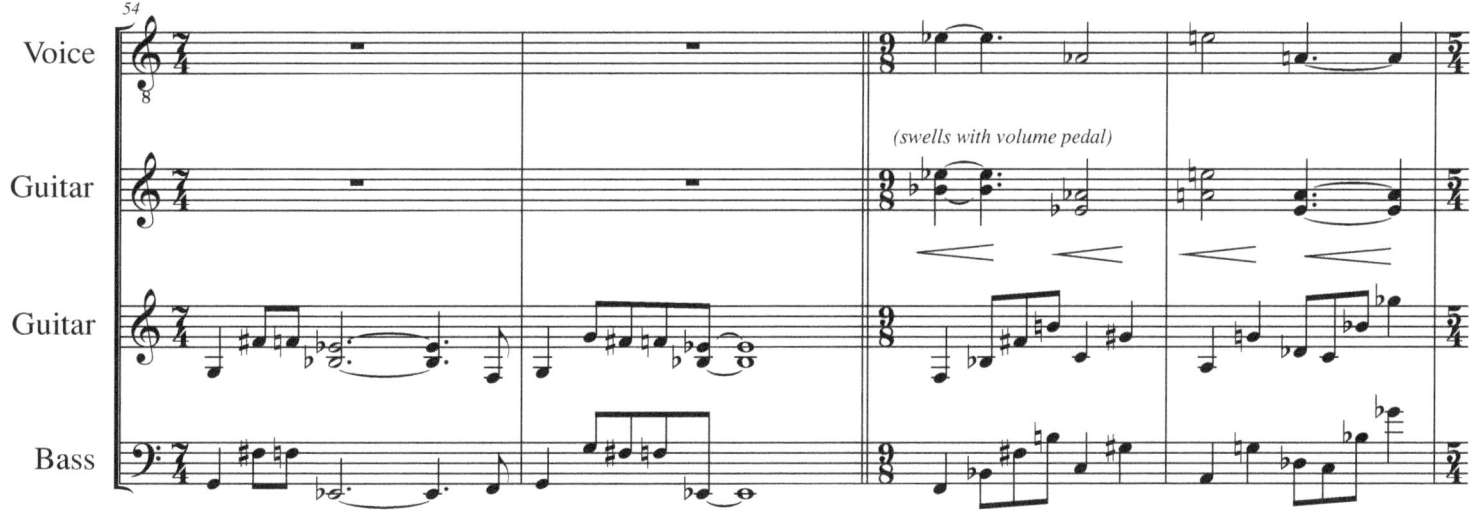

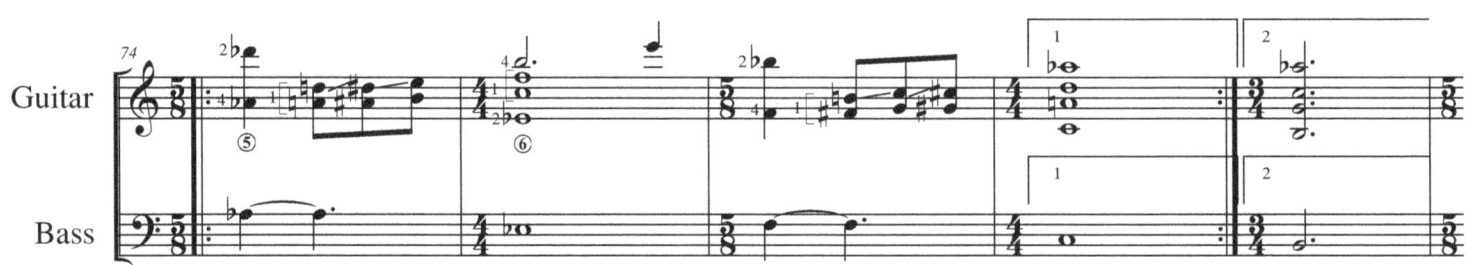

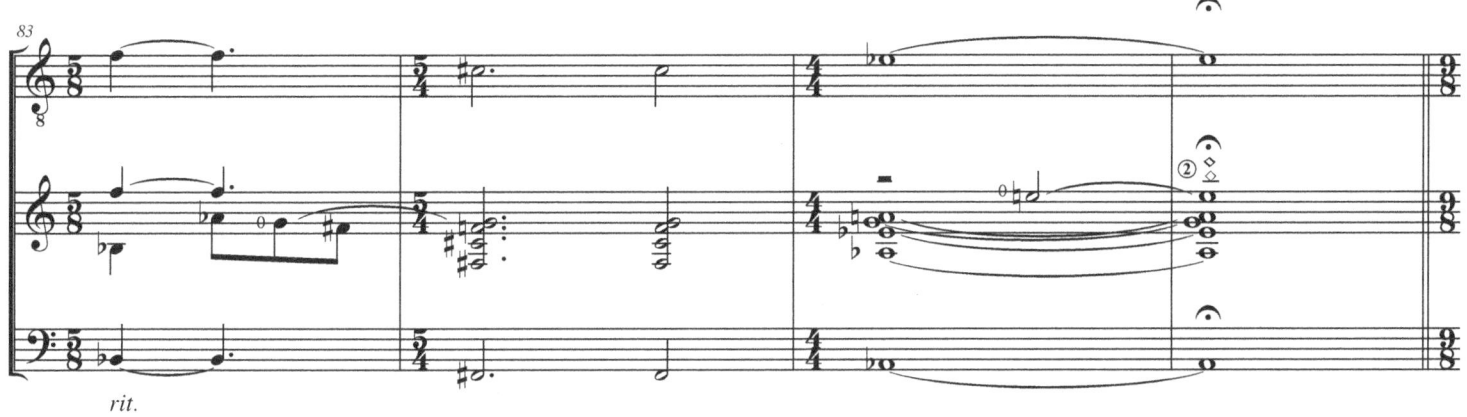

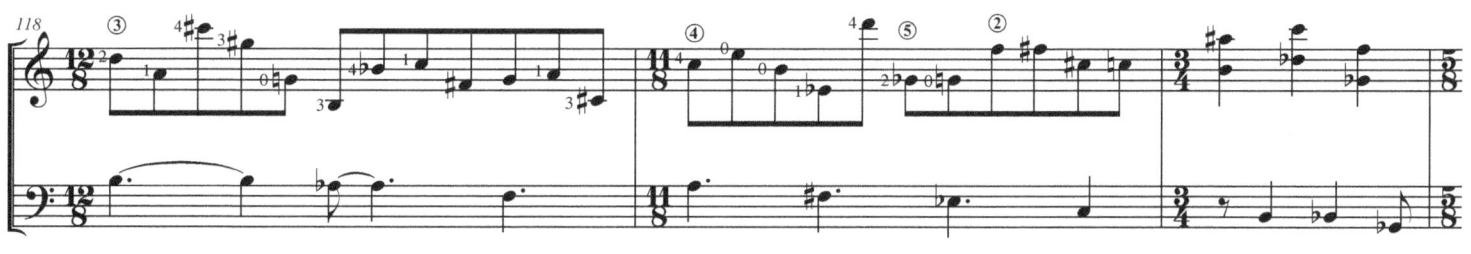

173
173
177
177
182
186
186

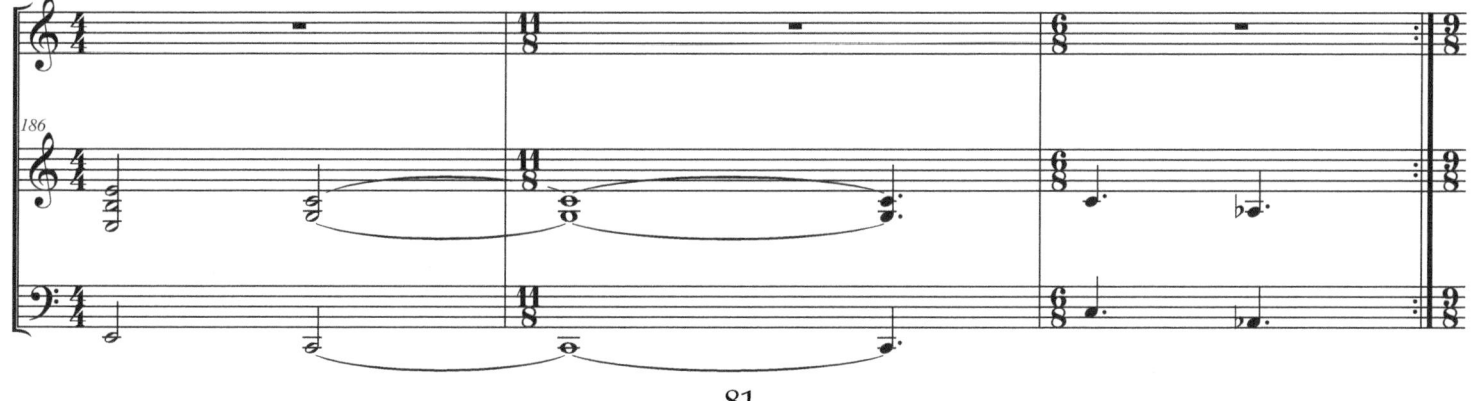

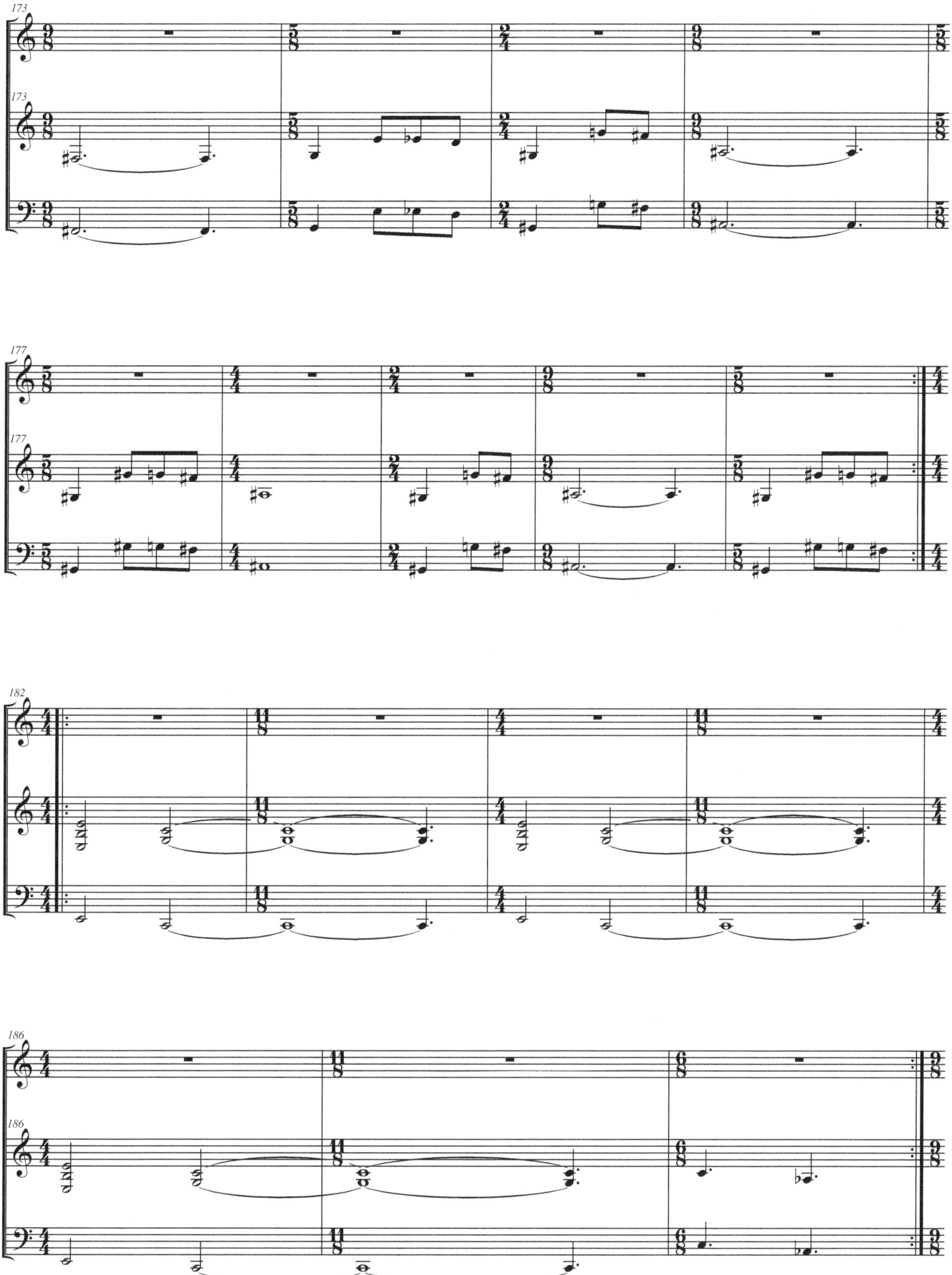

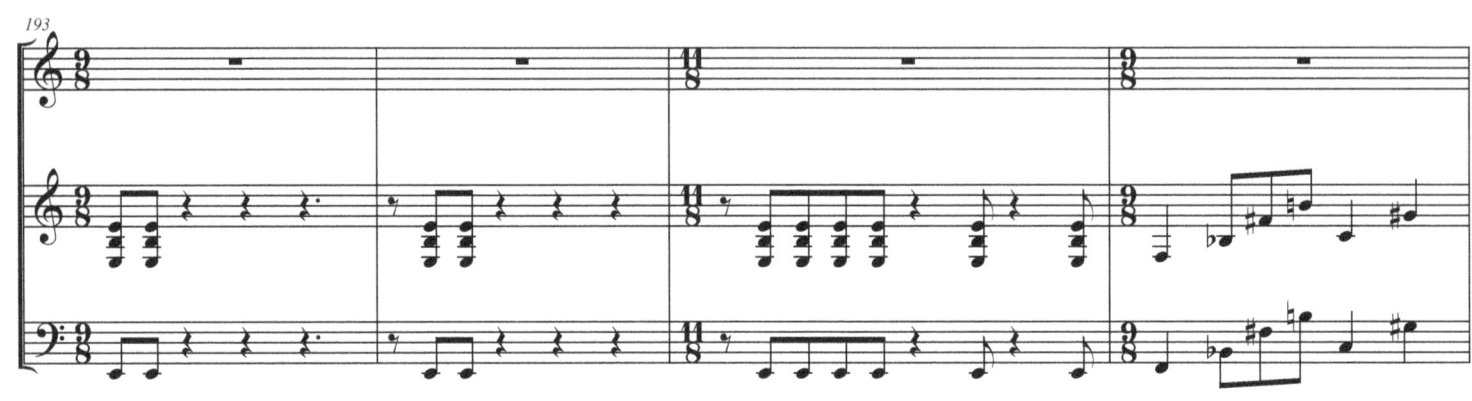

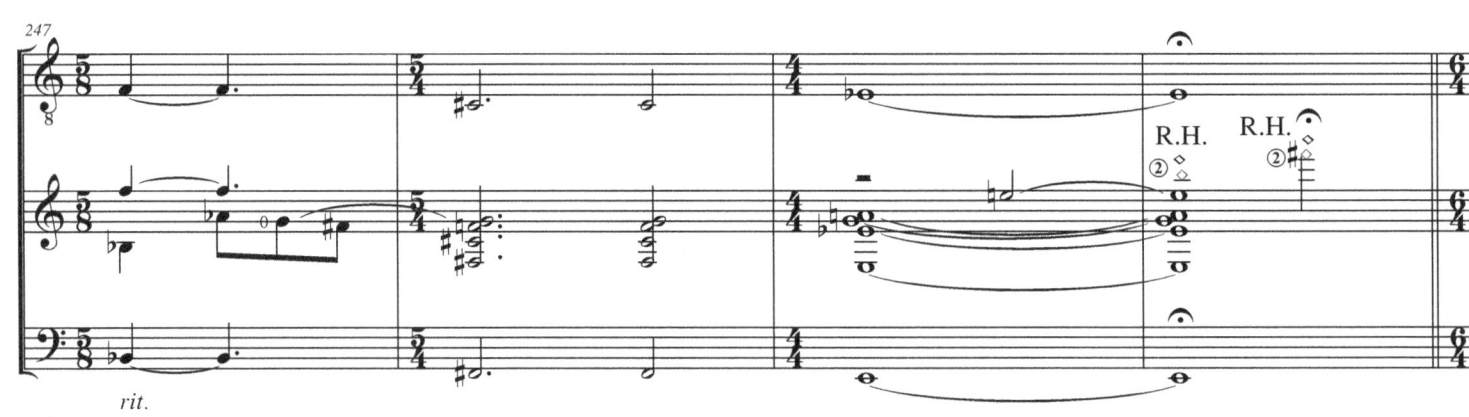

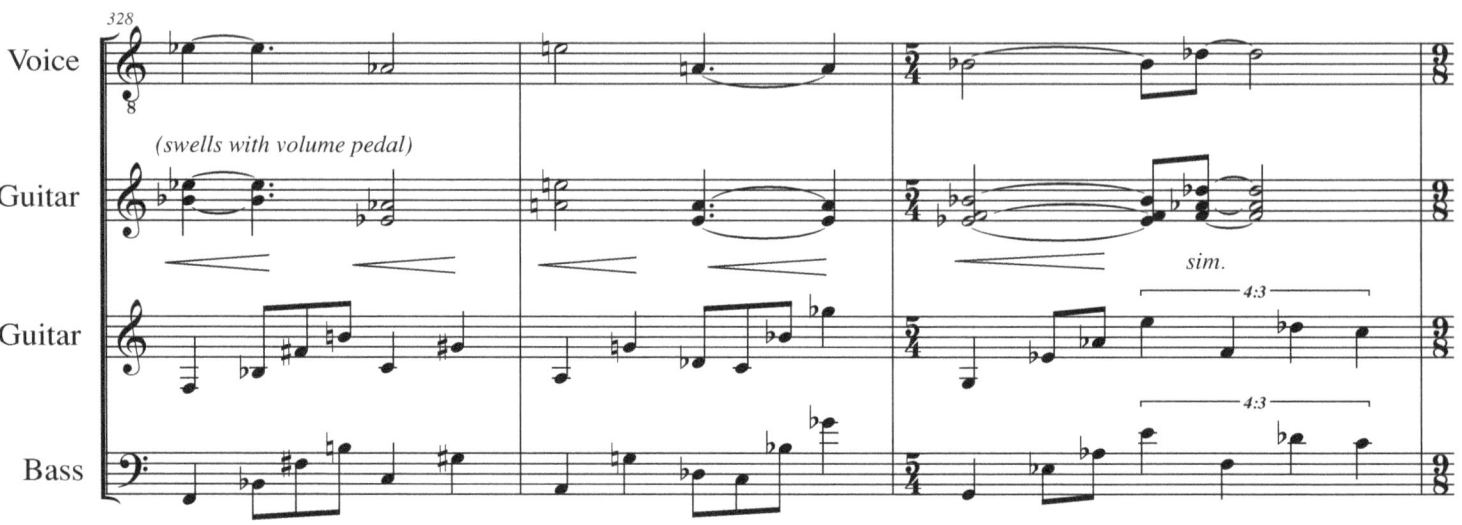

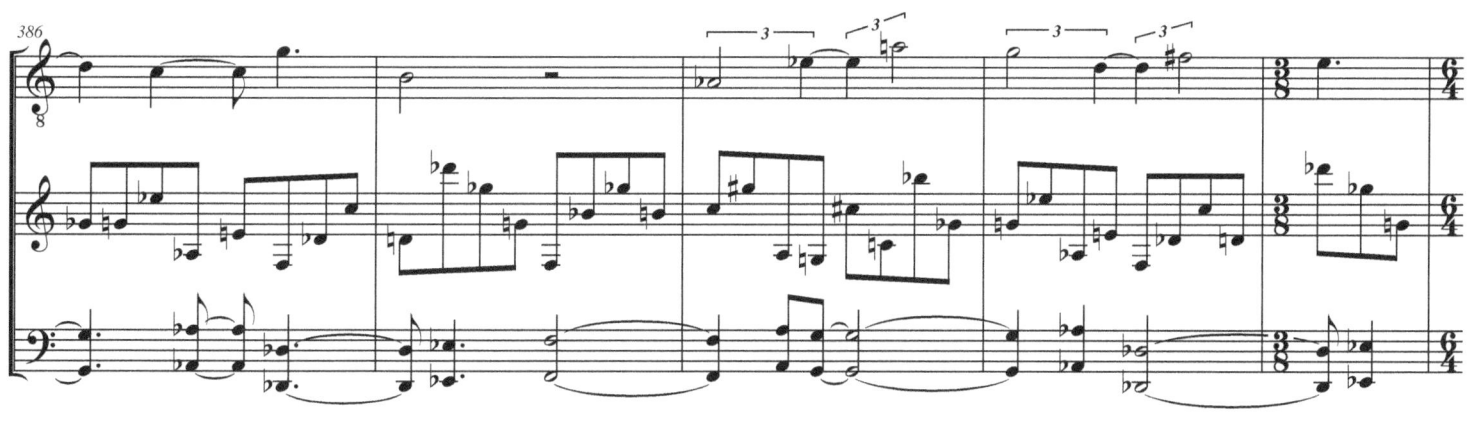

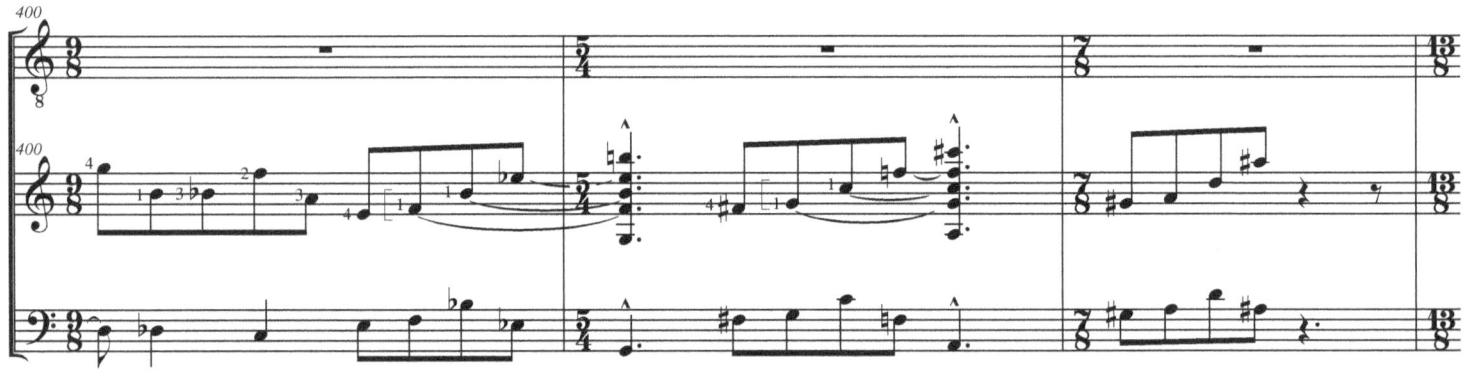

In Memoriam

Ben Monder

Luteous Pangolin

Ben Monder

Mistral

Ben Monder

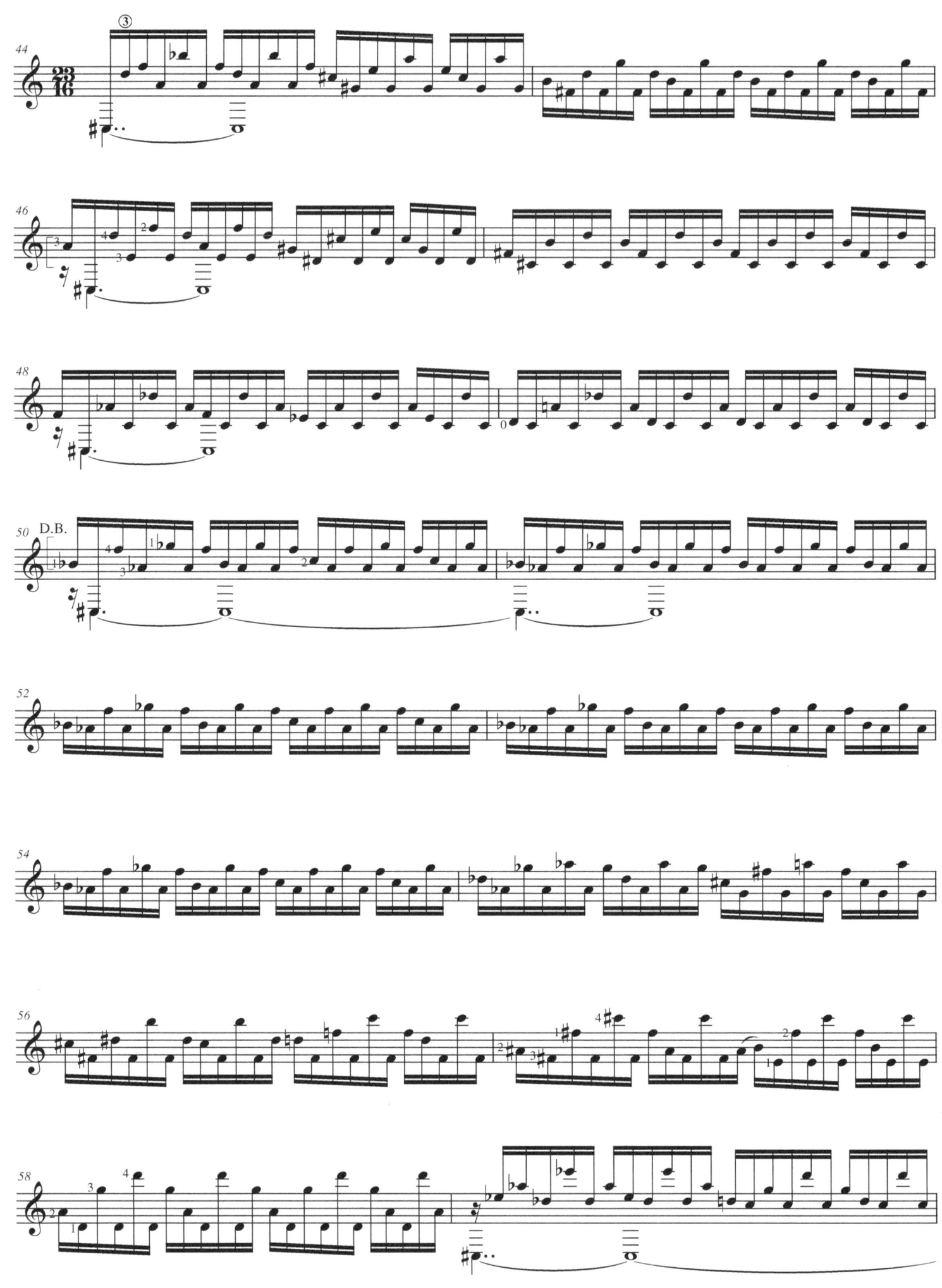

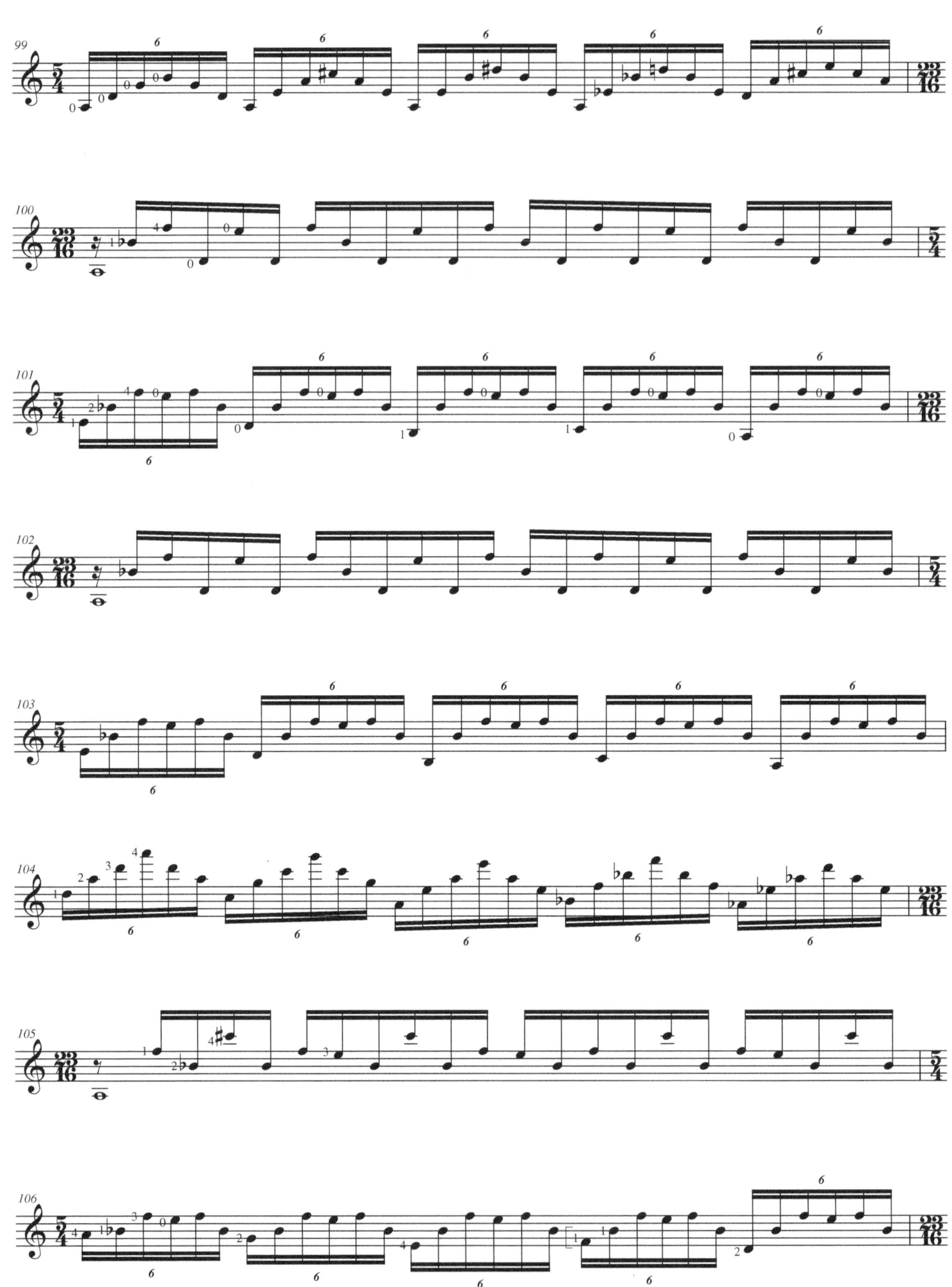

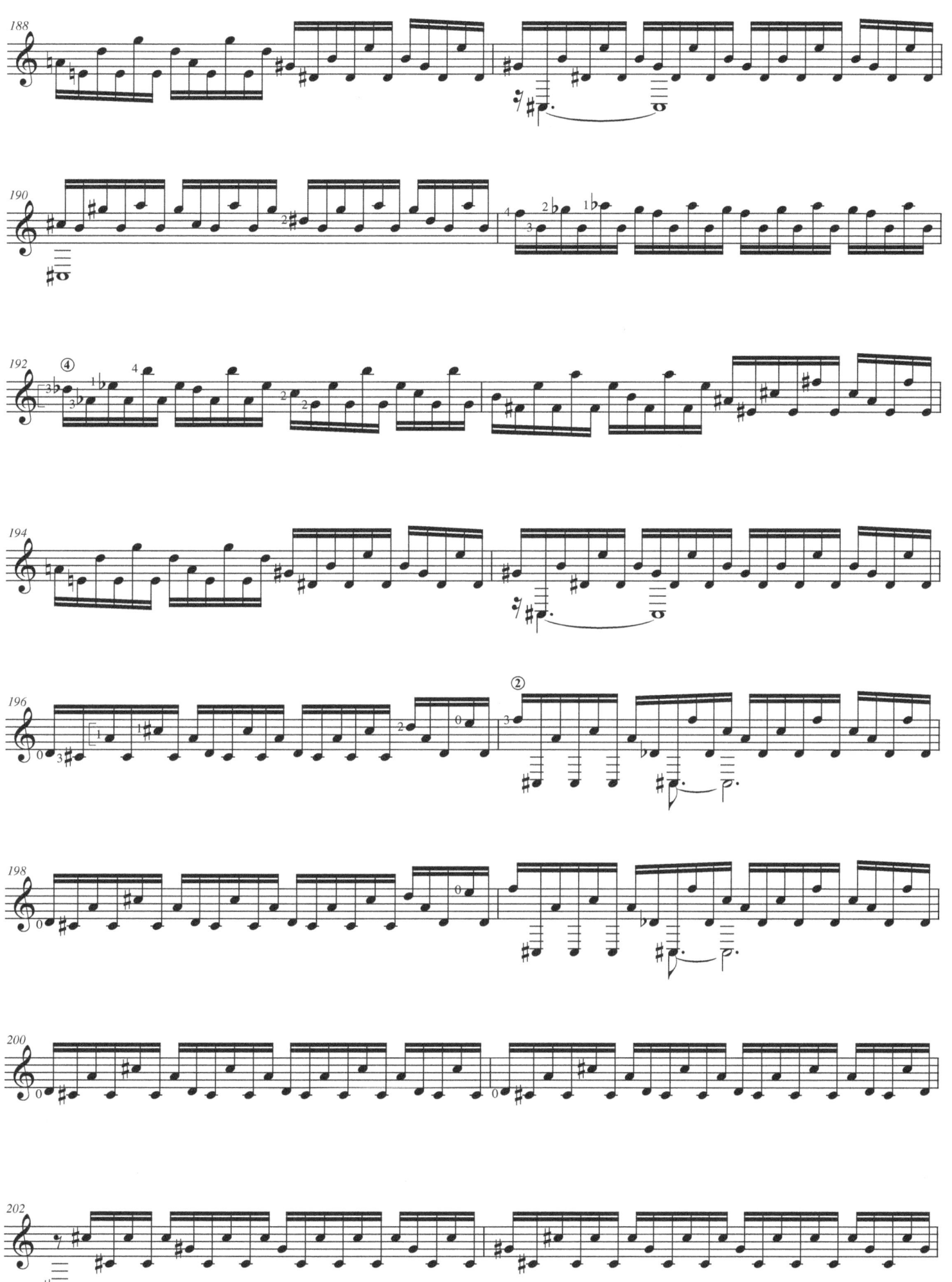

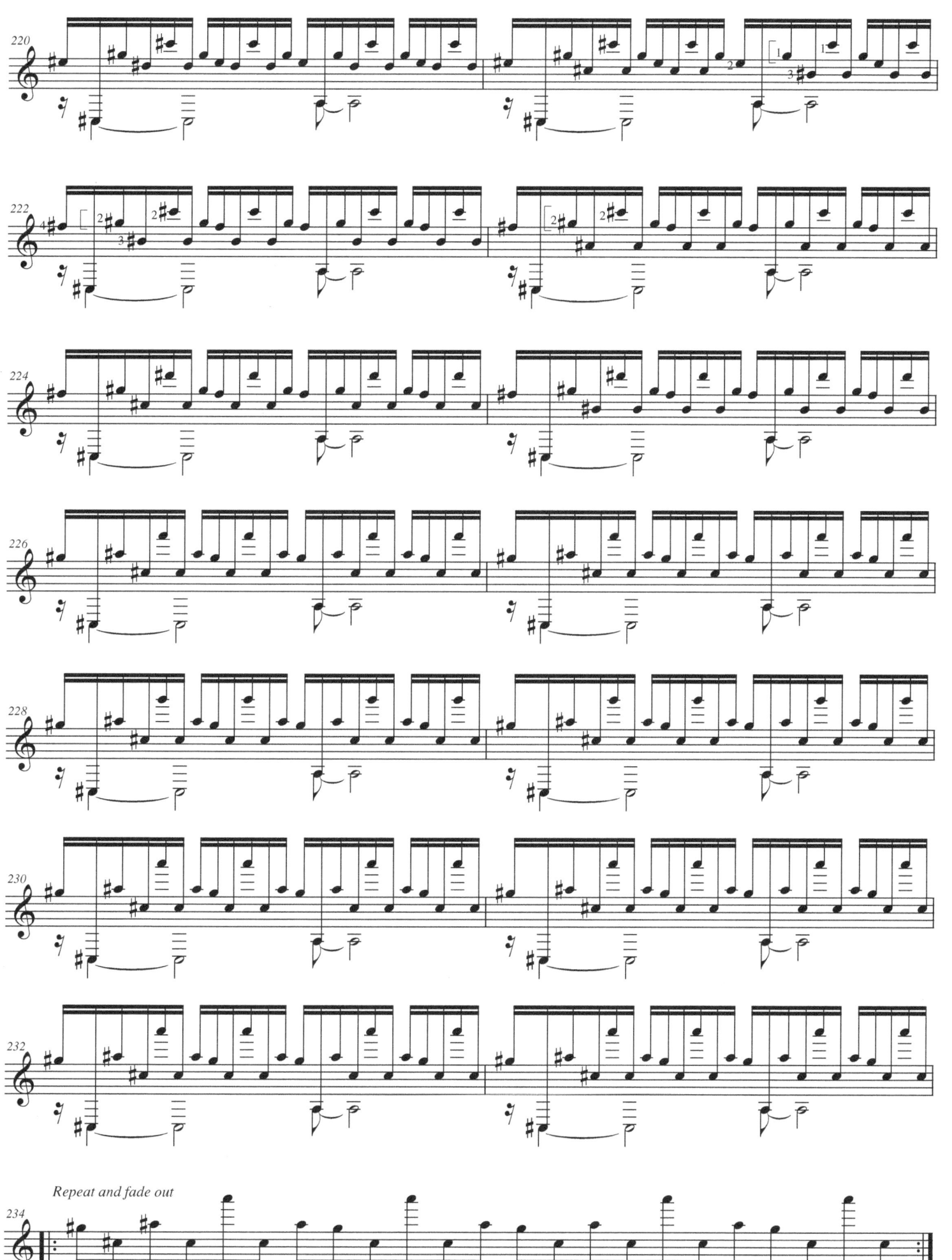

Muvseevum

Ben Monder

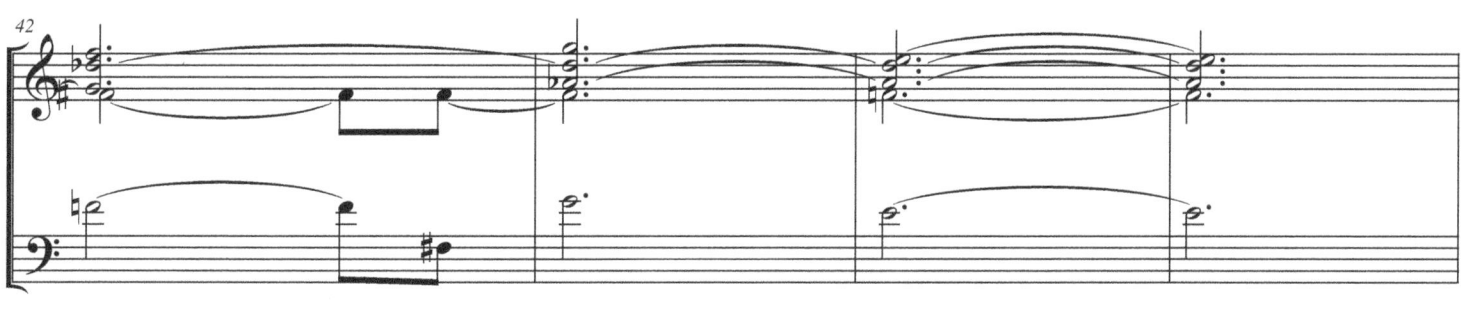

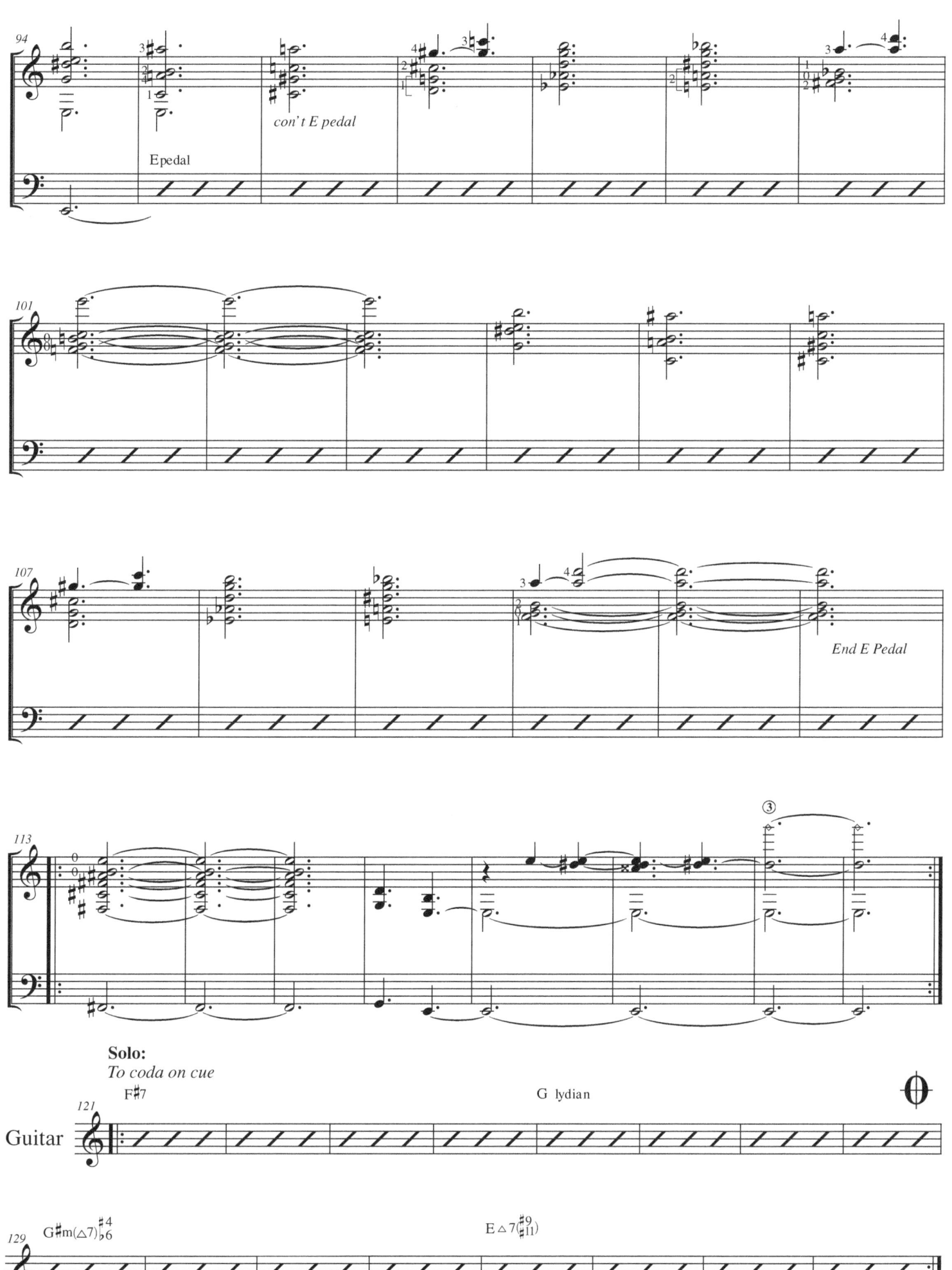

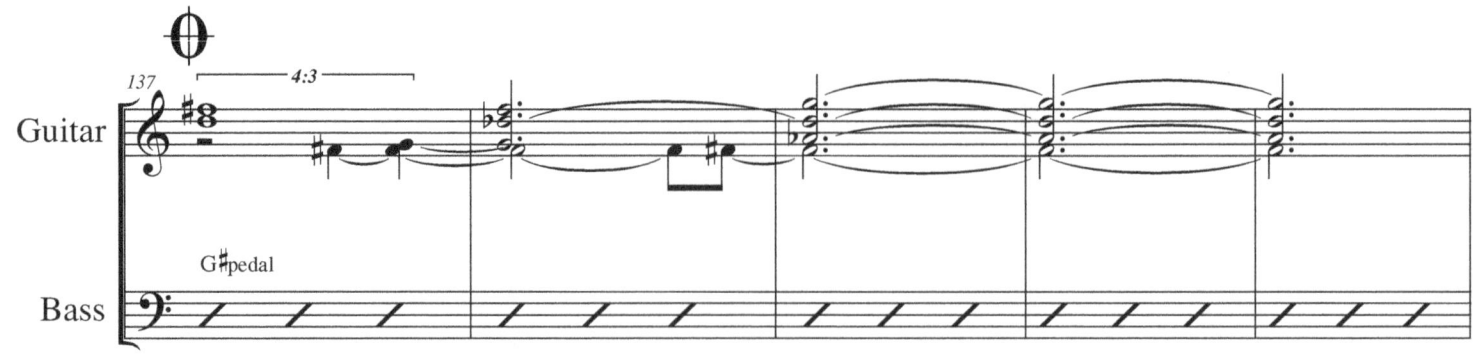

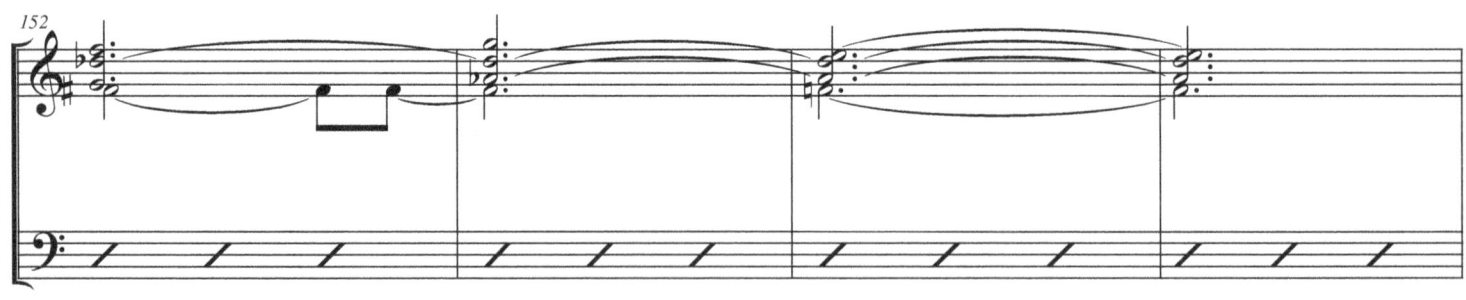

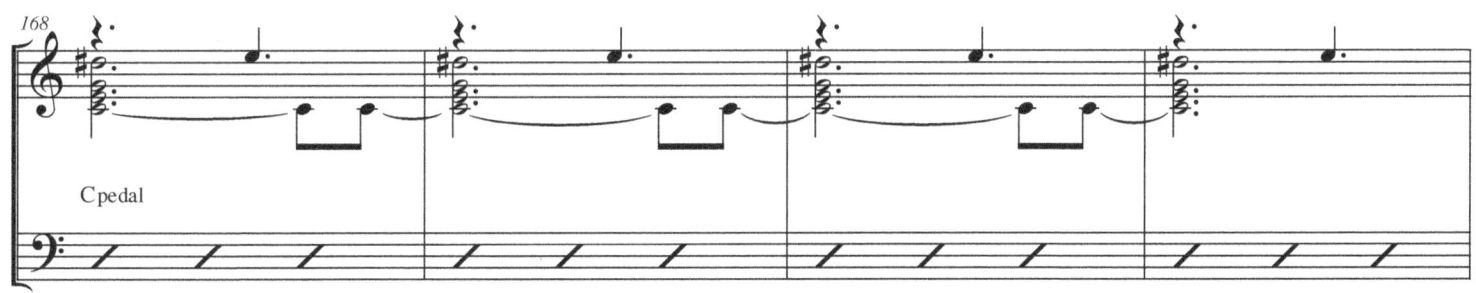
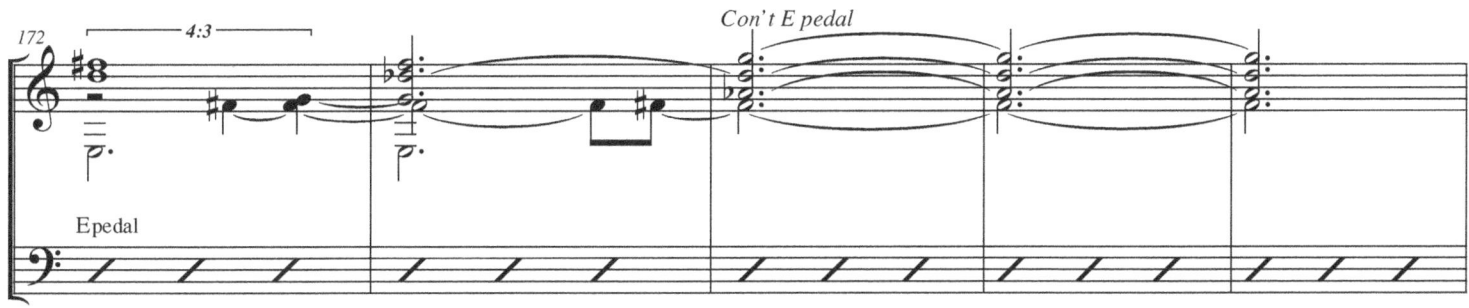
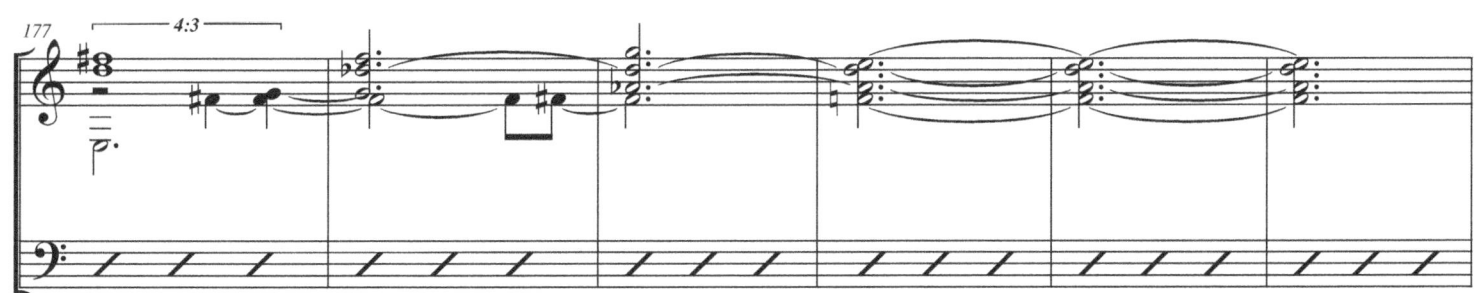

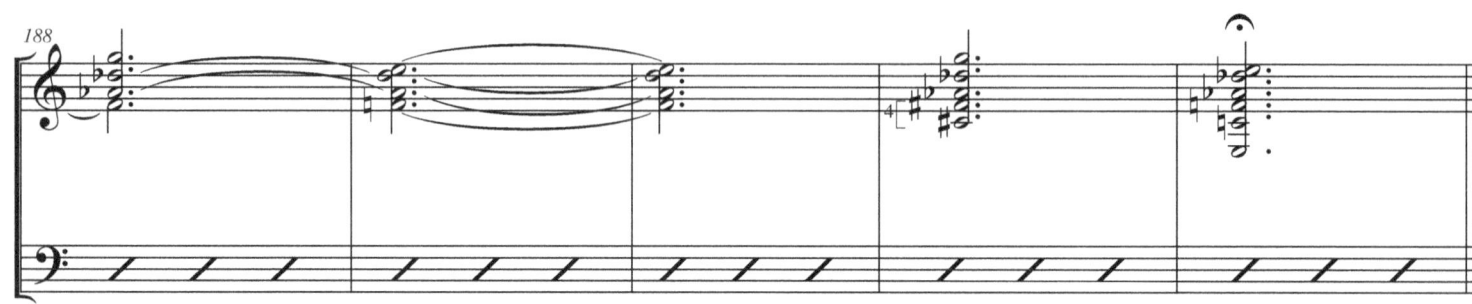

Oceana

Ben Monder

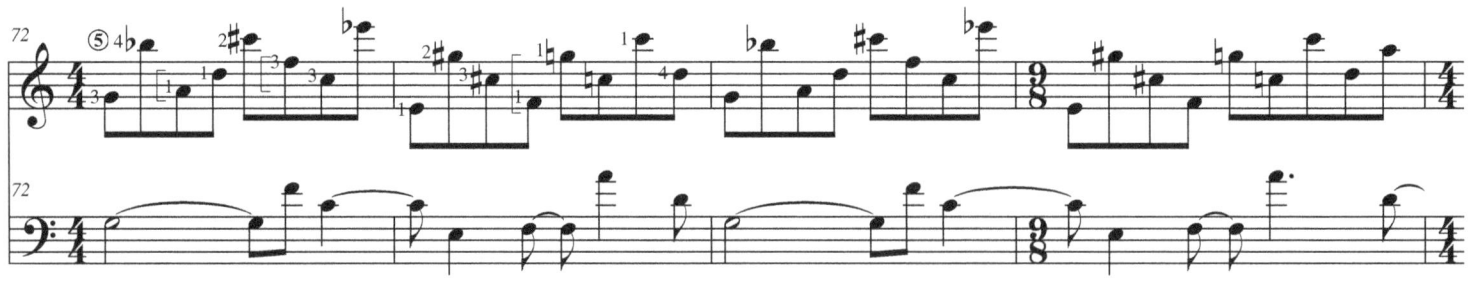

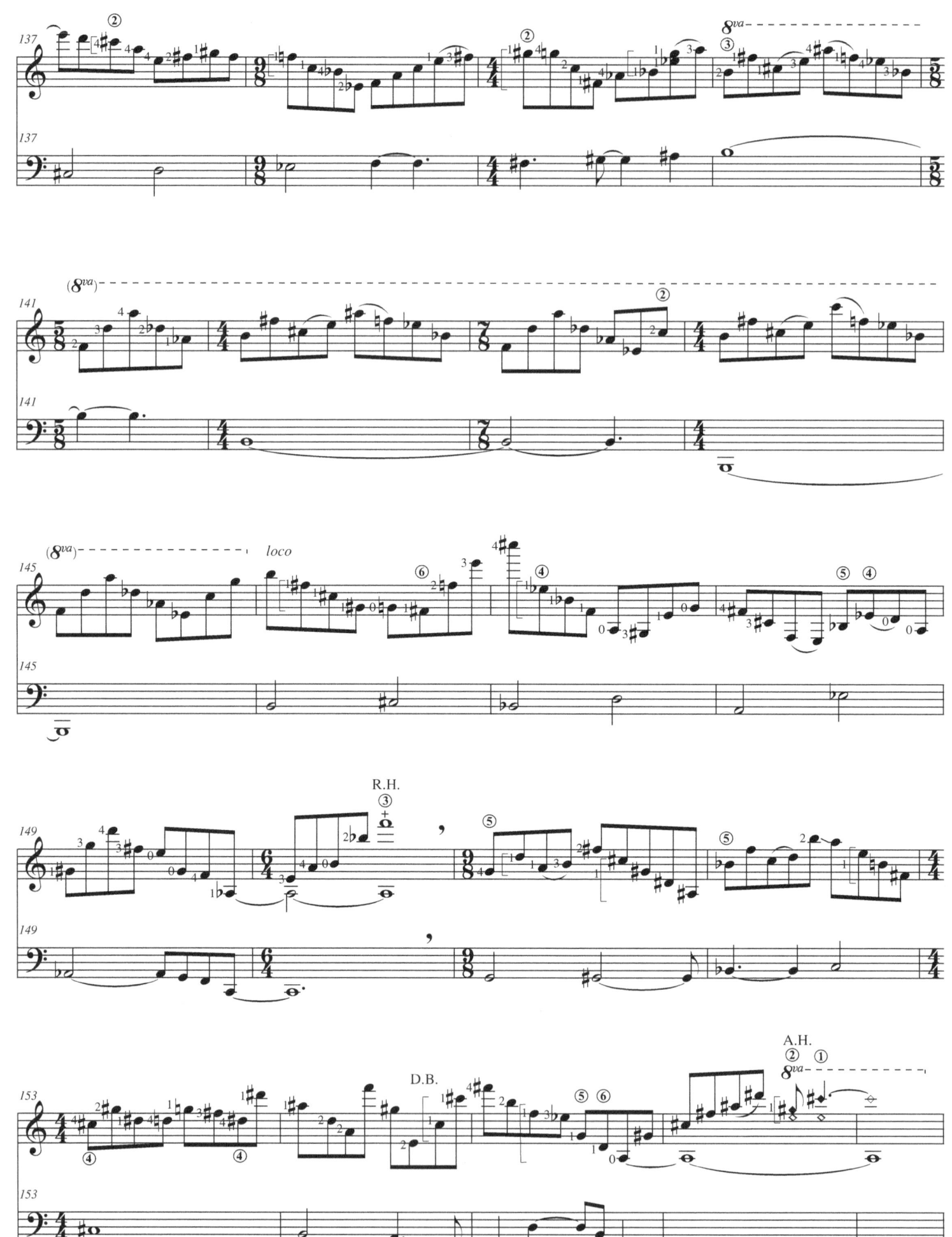

pp
T
ad lib strum
Guitar
A - △7 (♭13 ♭9)/E
E♭- △7 (♯11 ♭9)/G♭
C - △7 (♭13 ♭9)/G

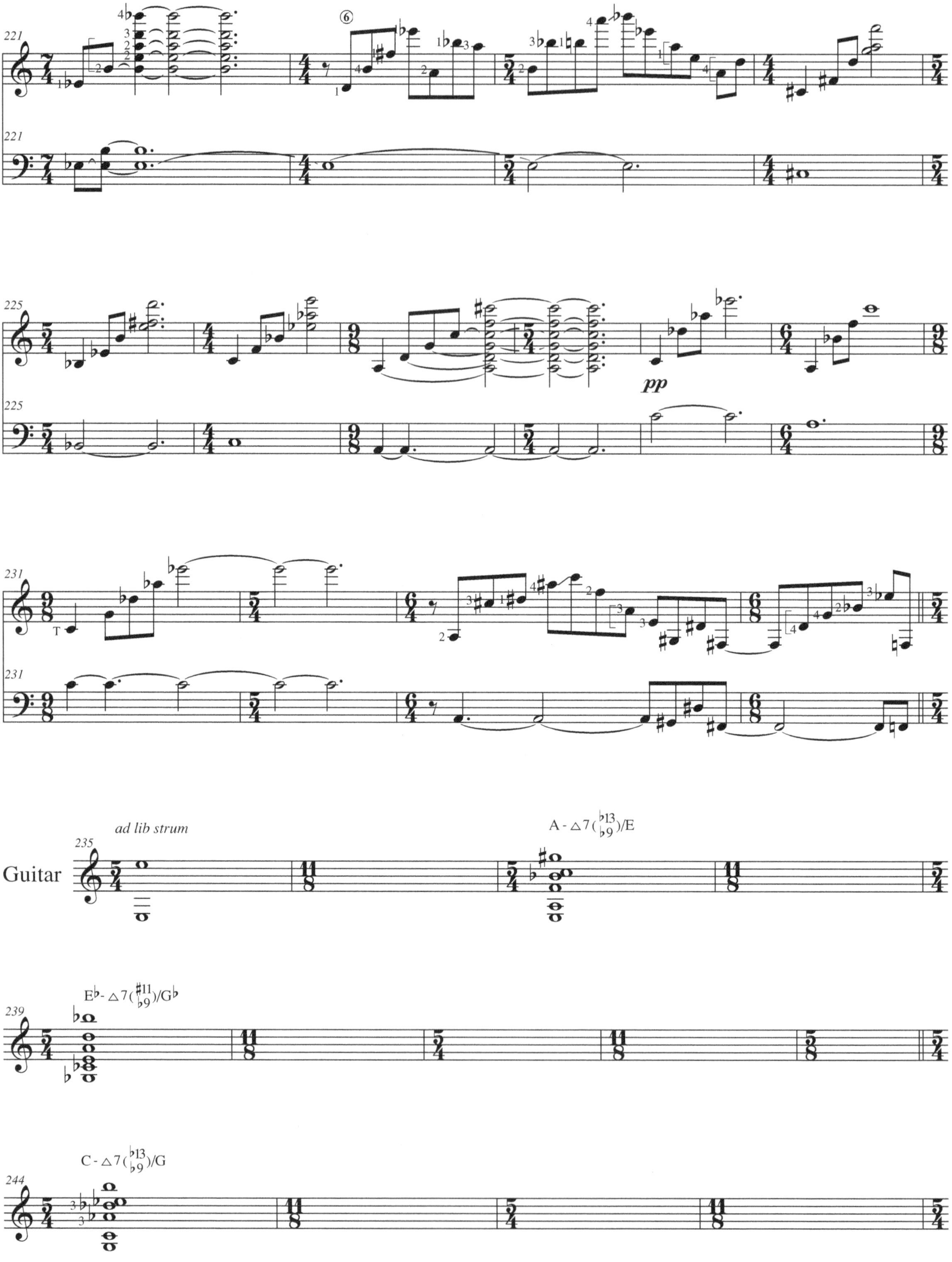

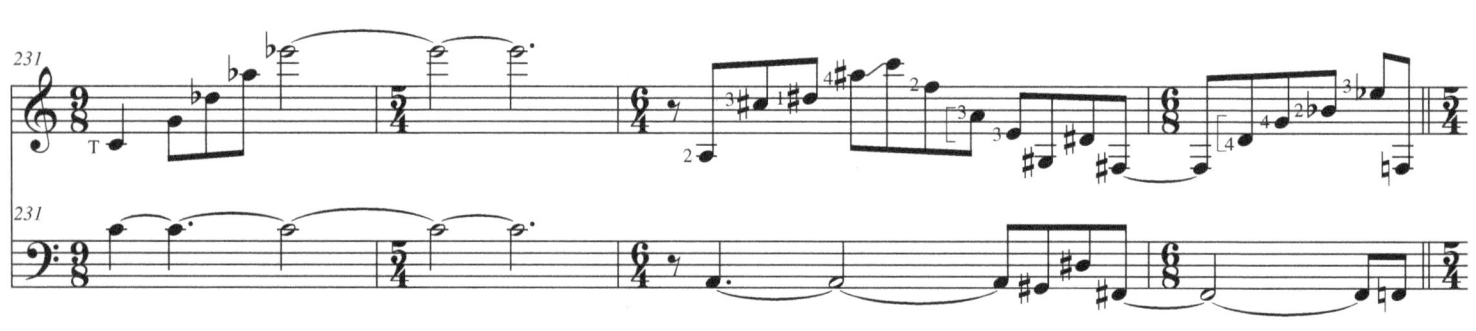

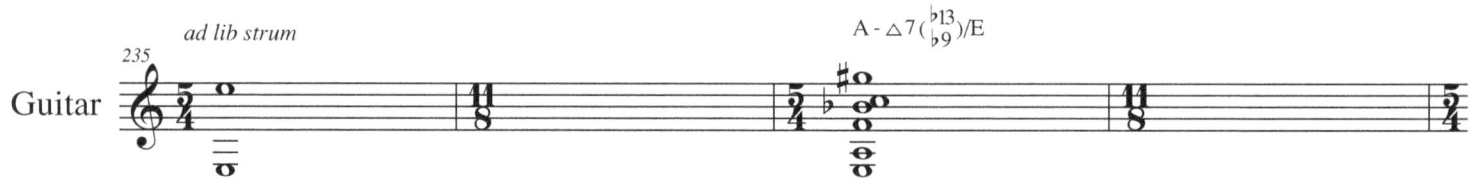

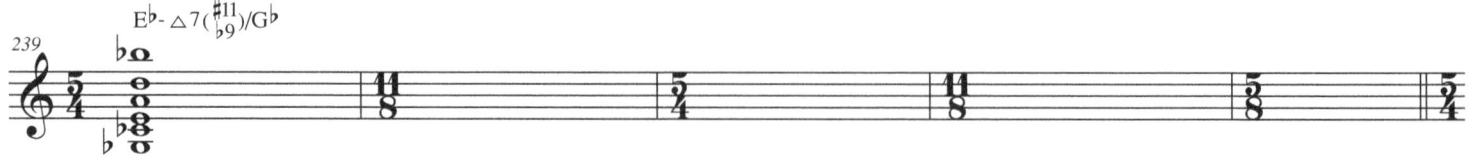

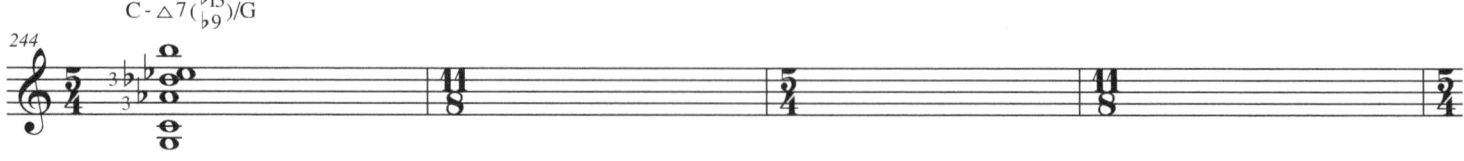

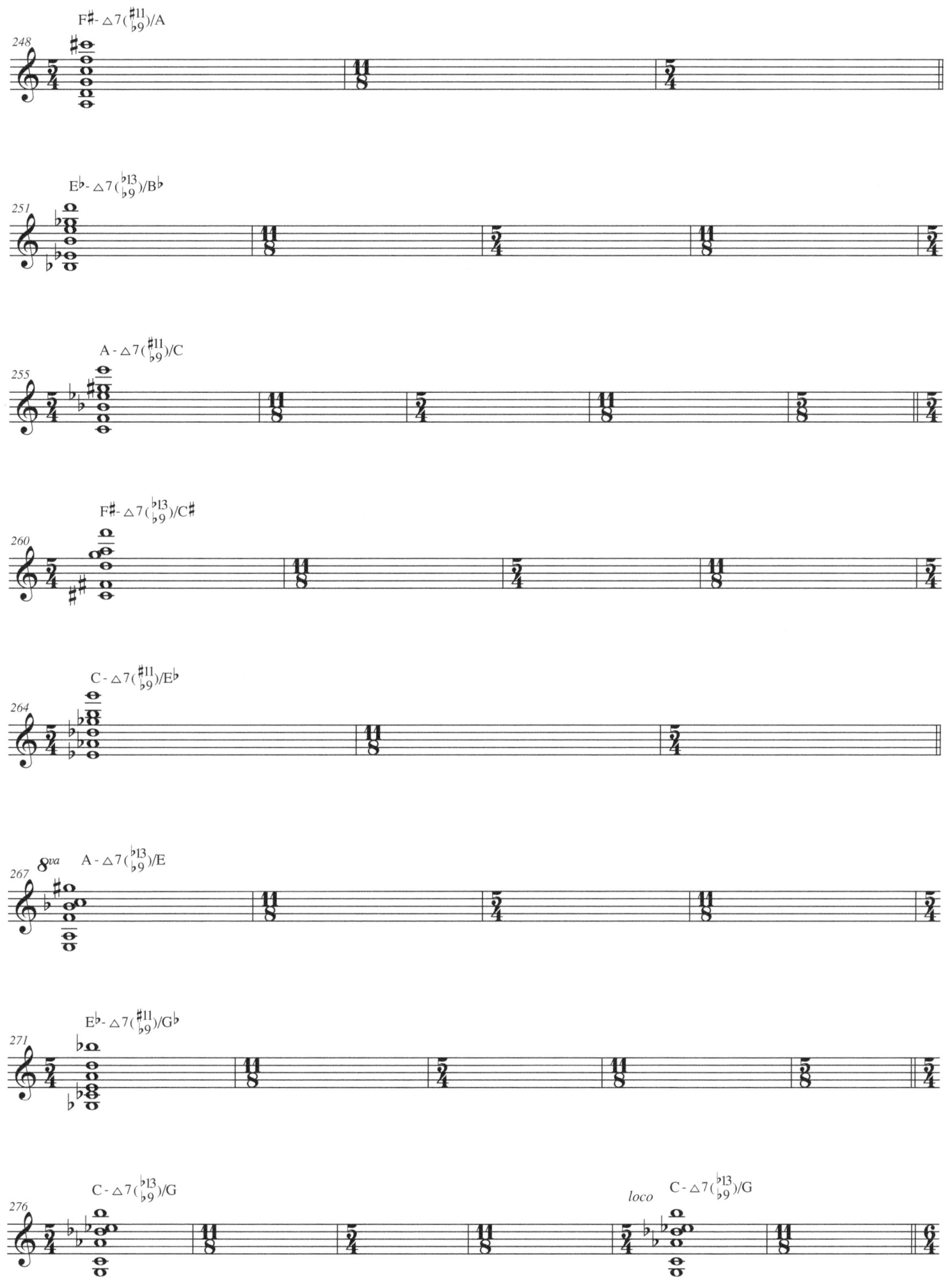

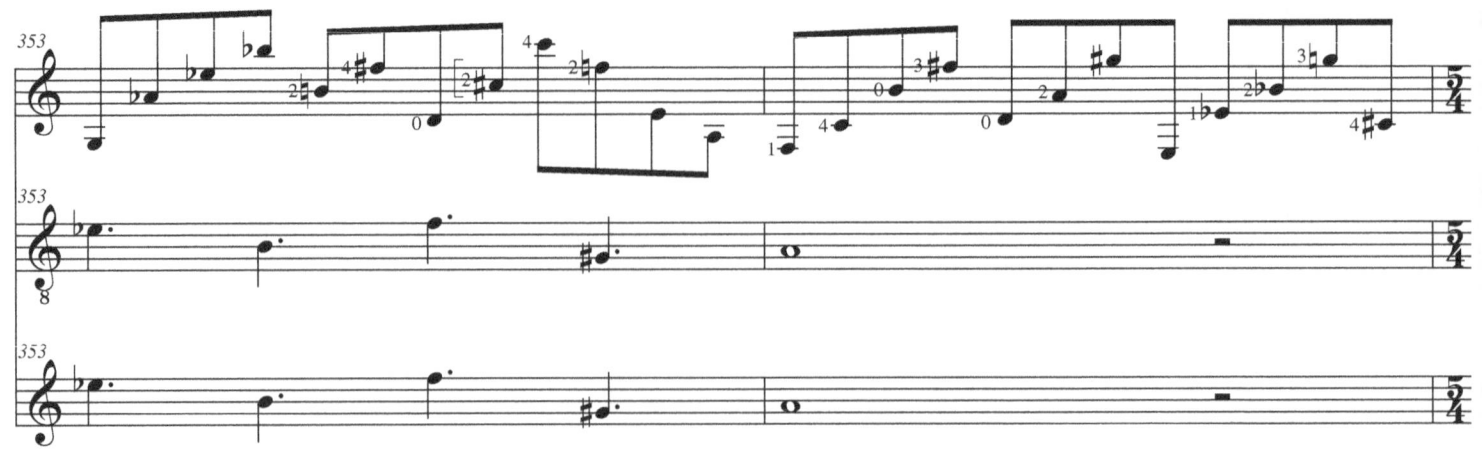

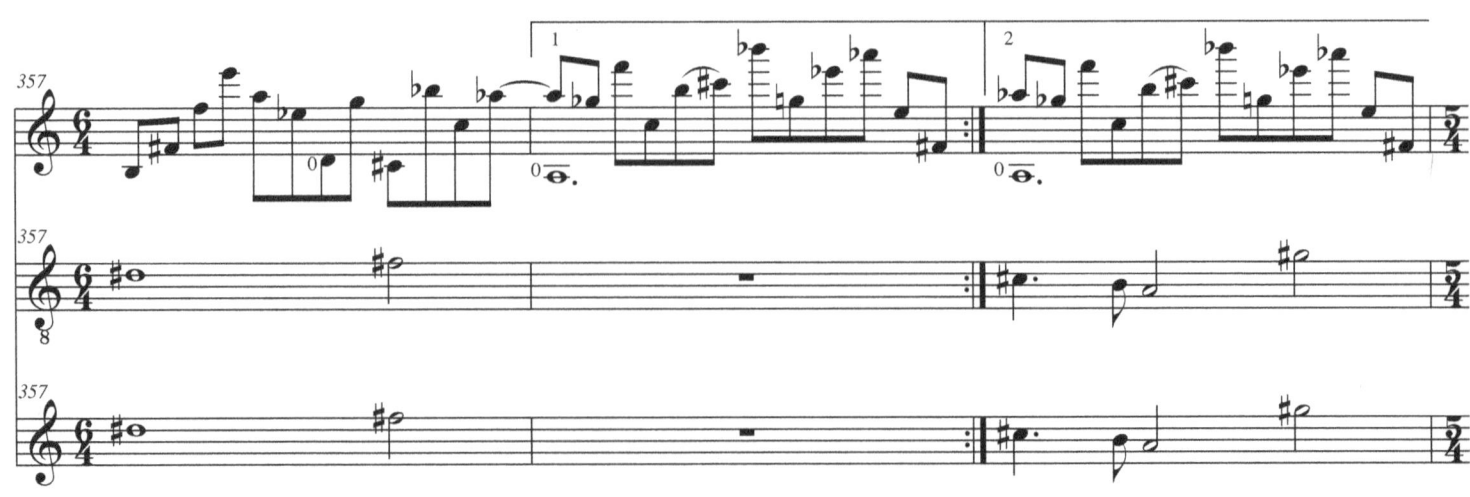

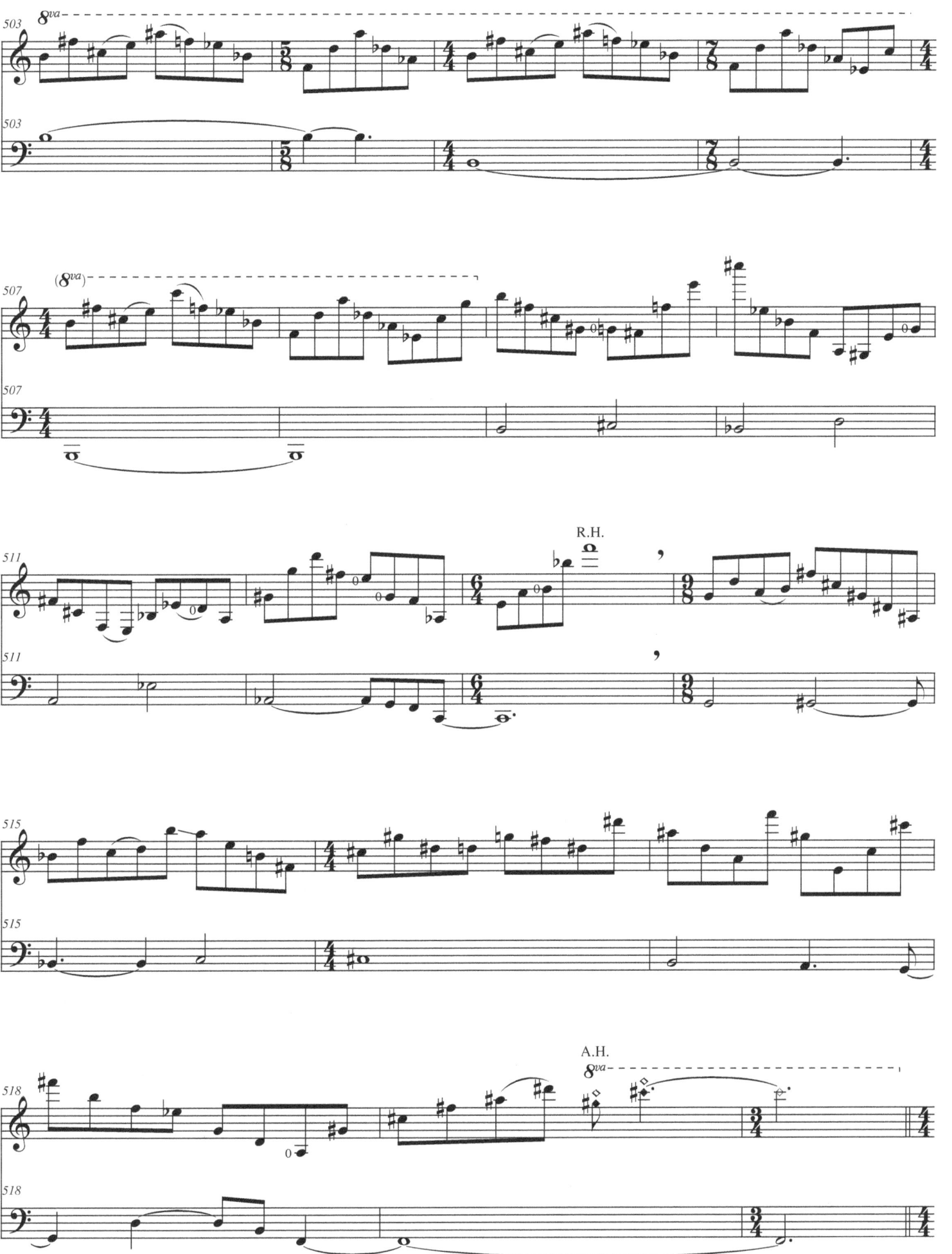

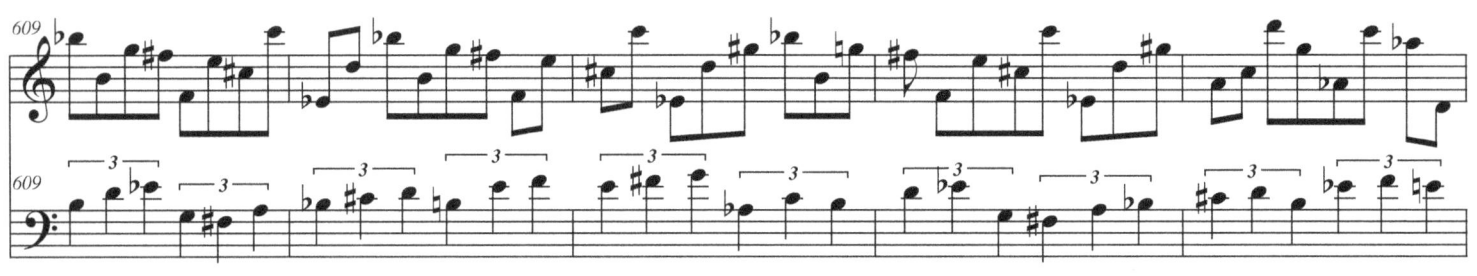
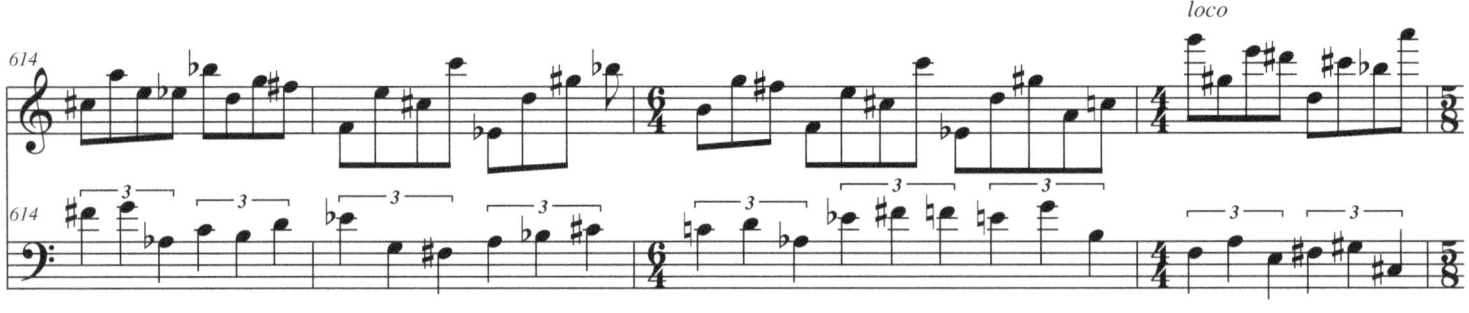
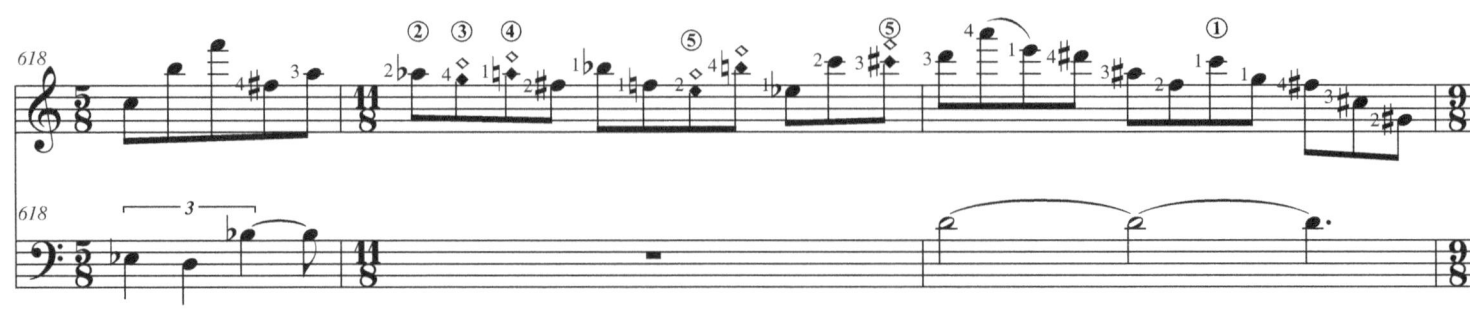

O.K. Chorale

Ben Monder

Orbits

Ben Monder

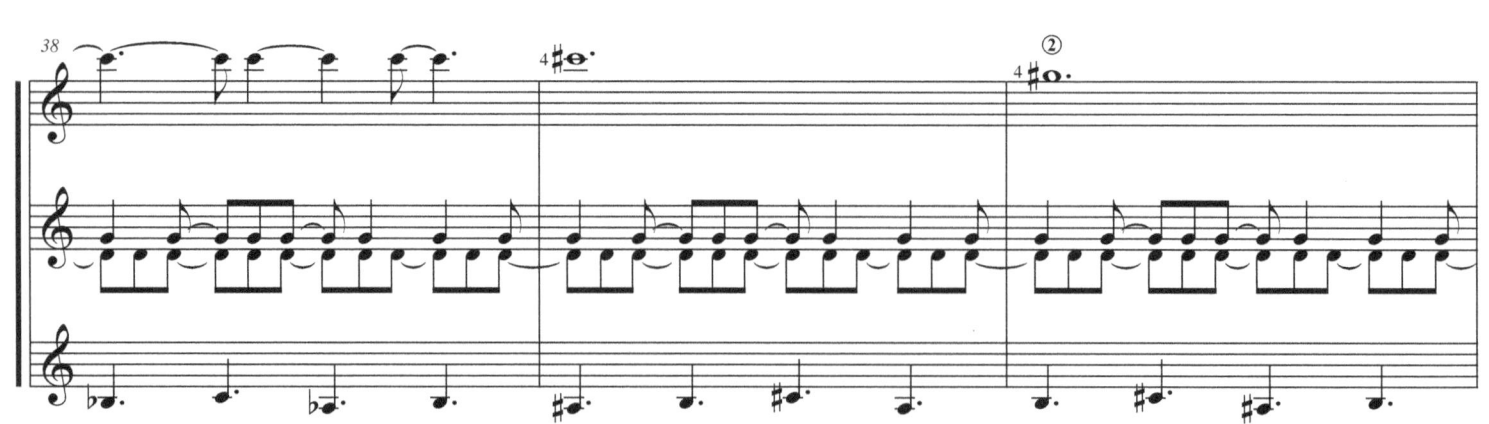

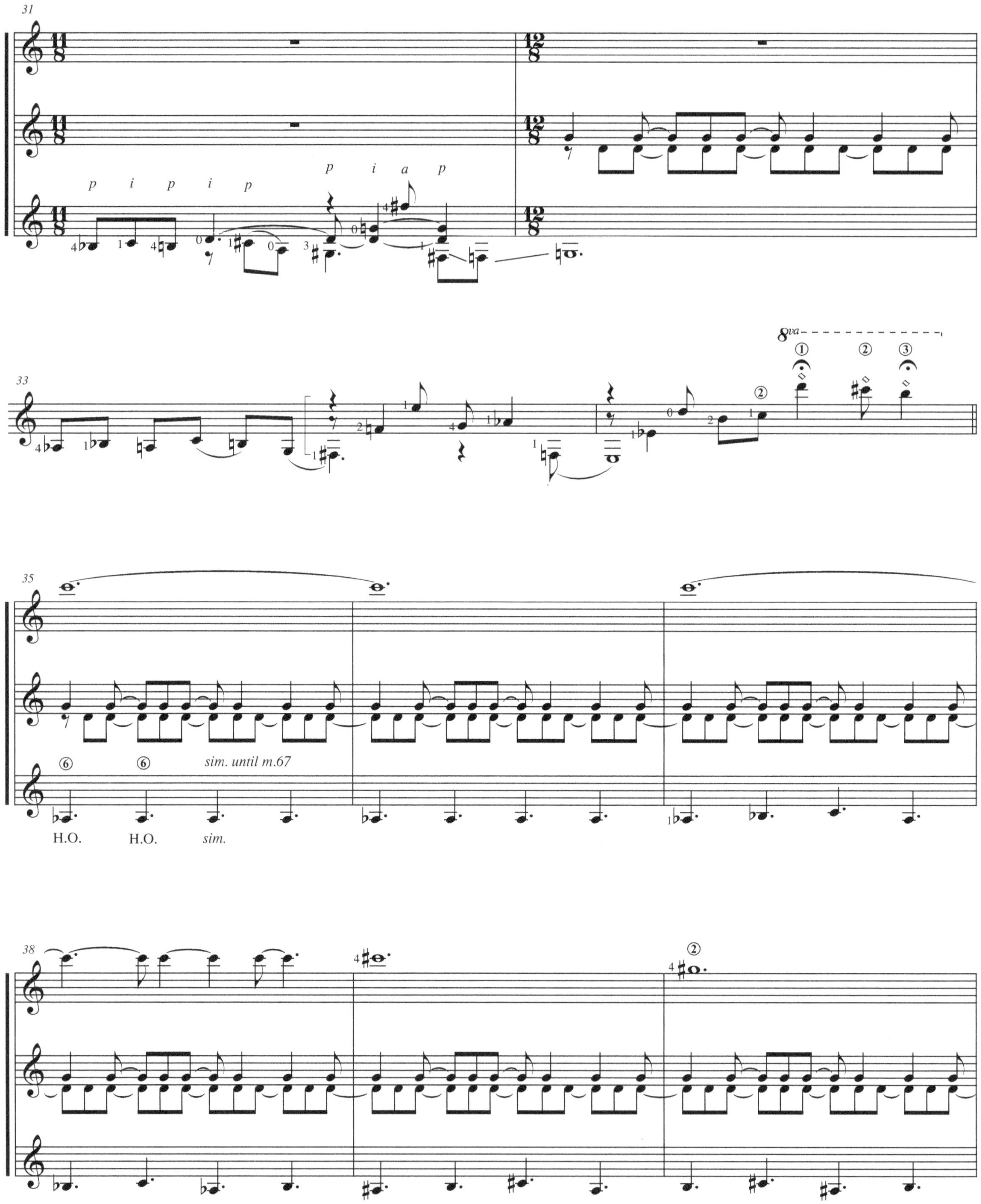
p i p i p
p i a p
8va
sim. until m.67
H.O.
H.O.
sim.

175

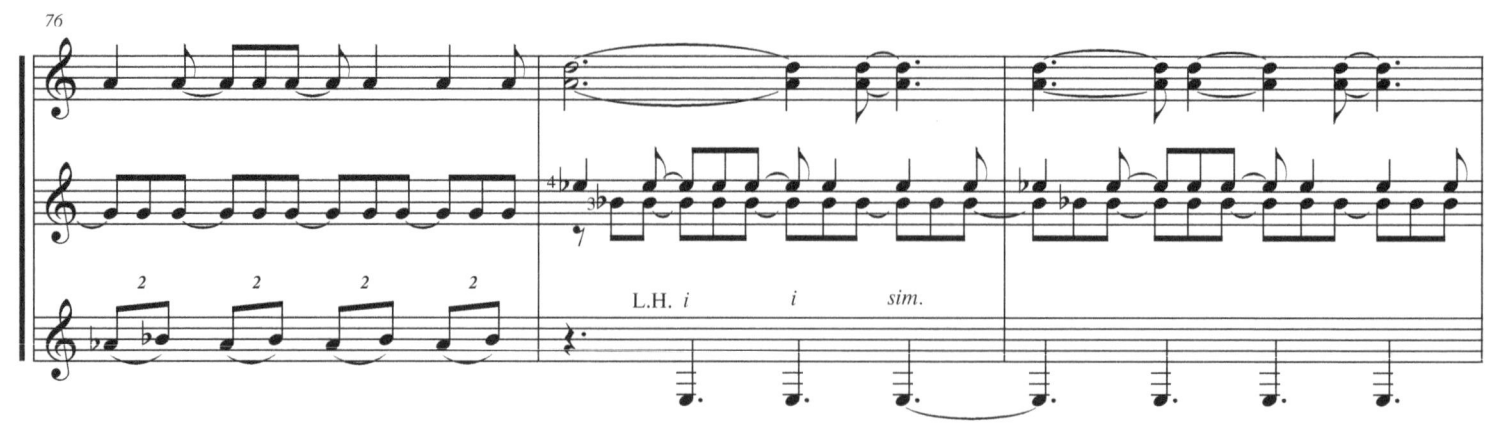

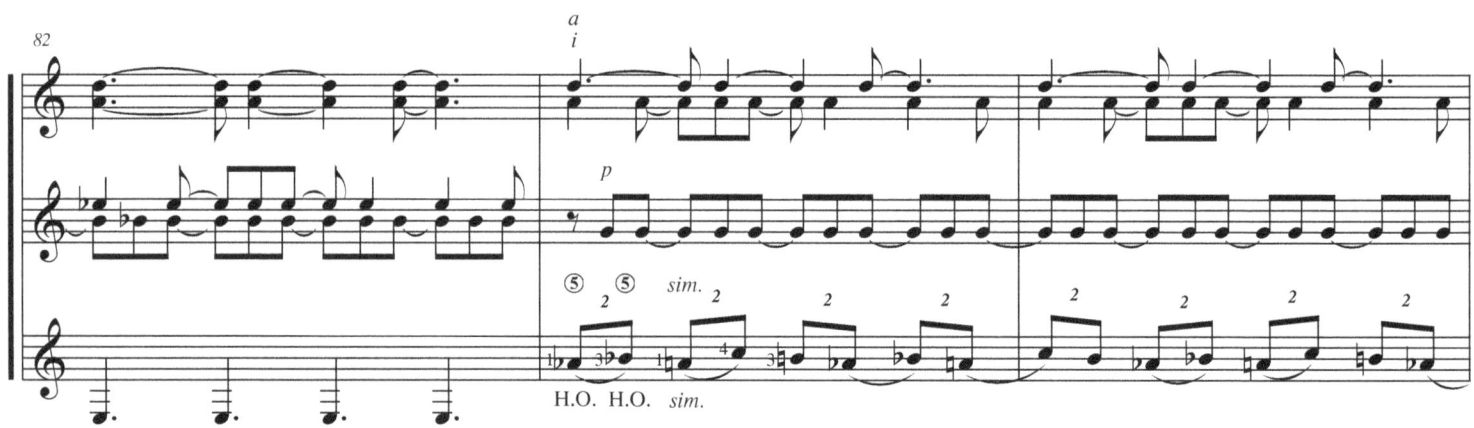

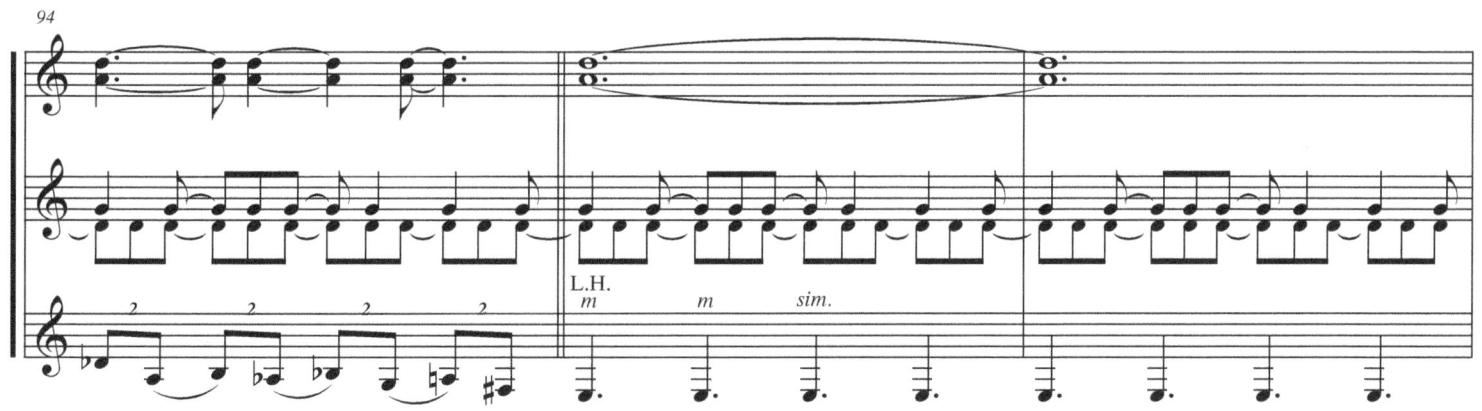

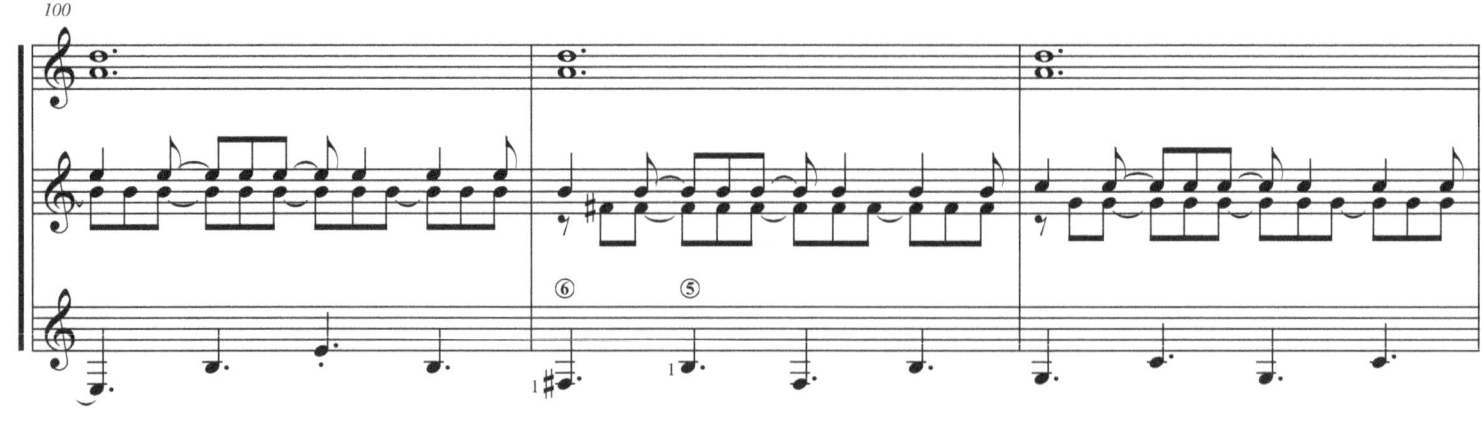

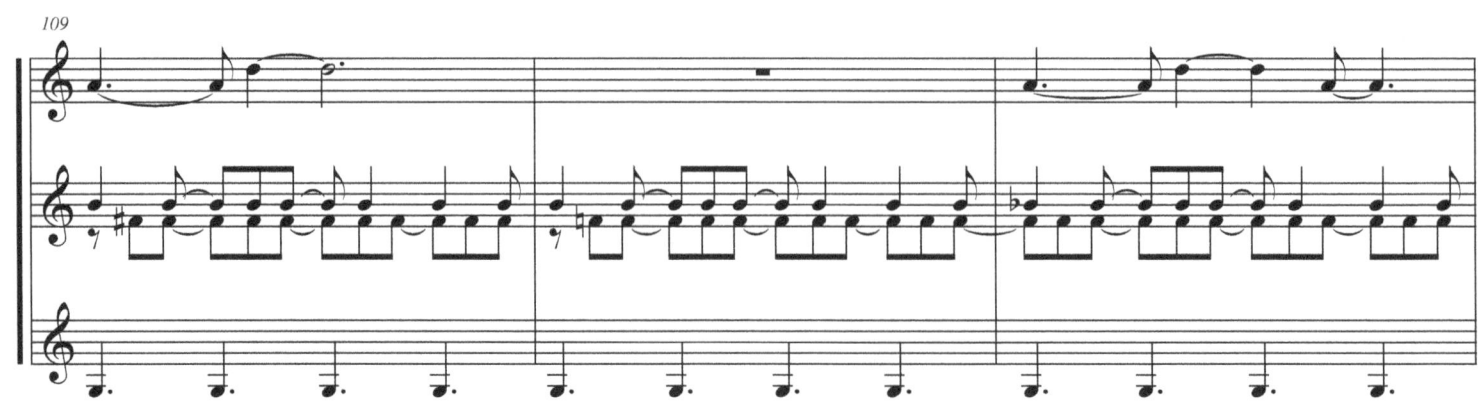

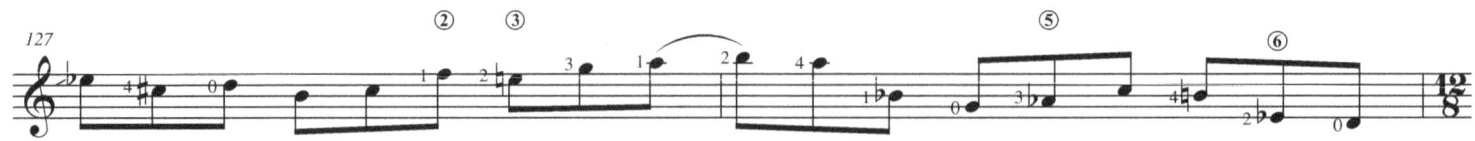

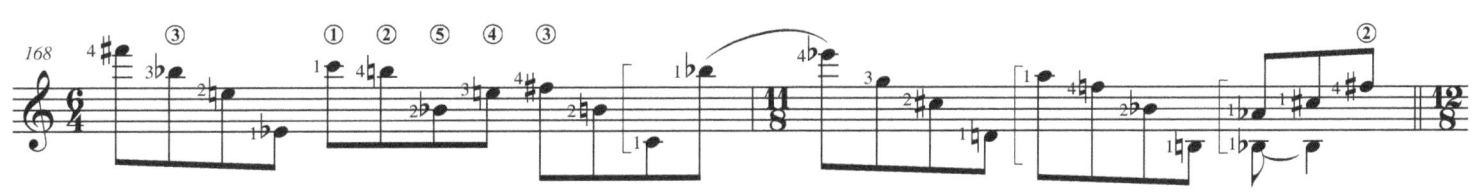
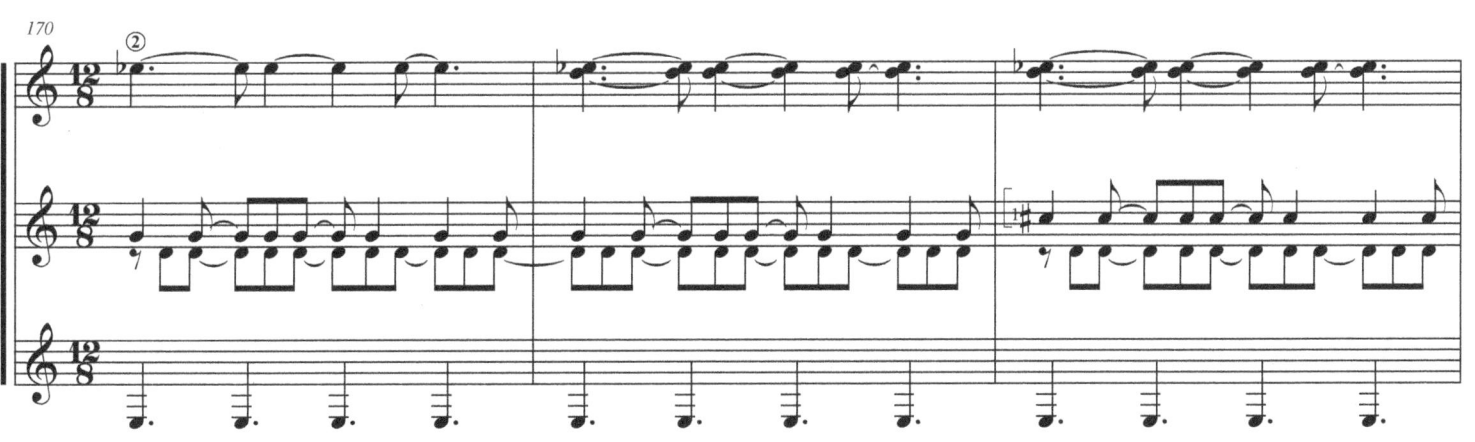

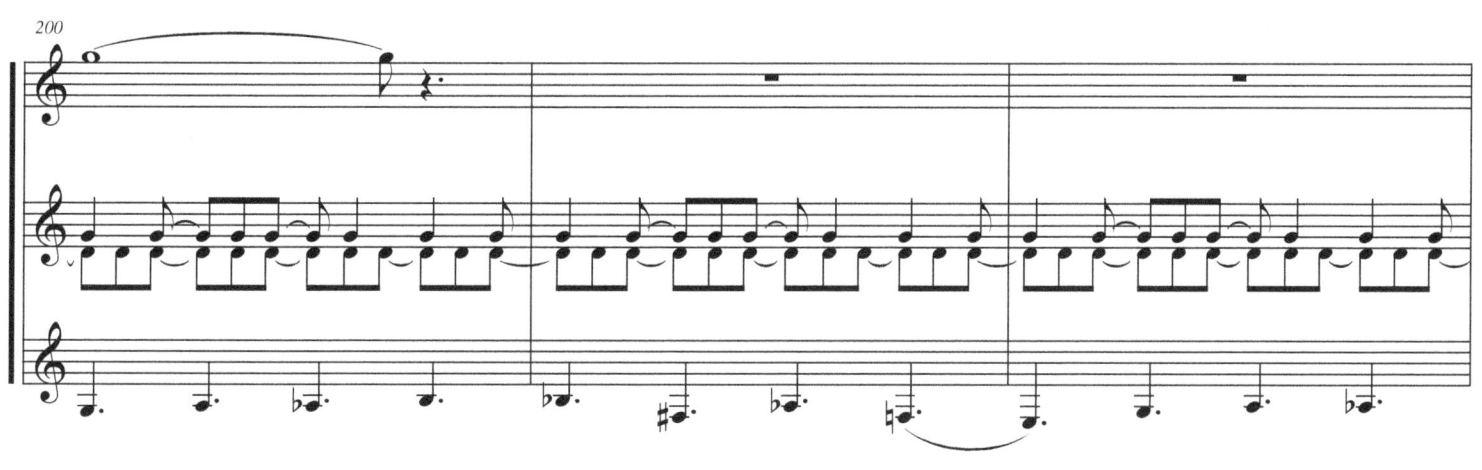

Propane Dream

Ben Monder

Red Shifts

Ben Monder

Rooms of Light

Ben Monder

201

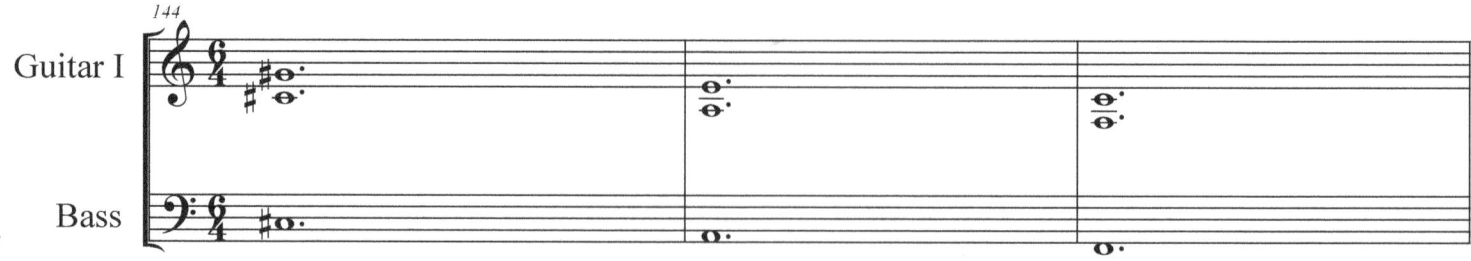

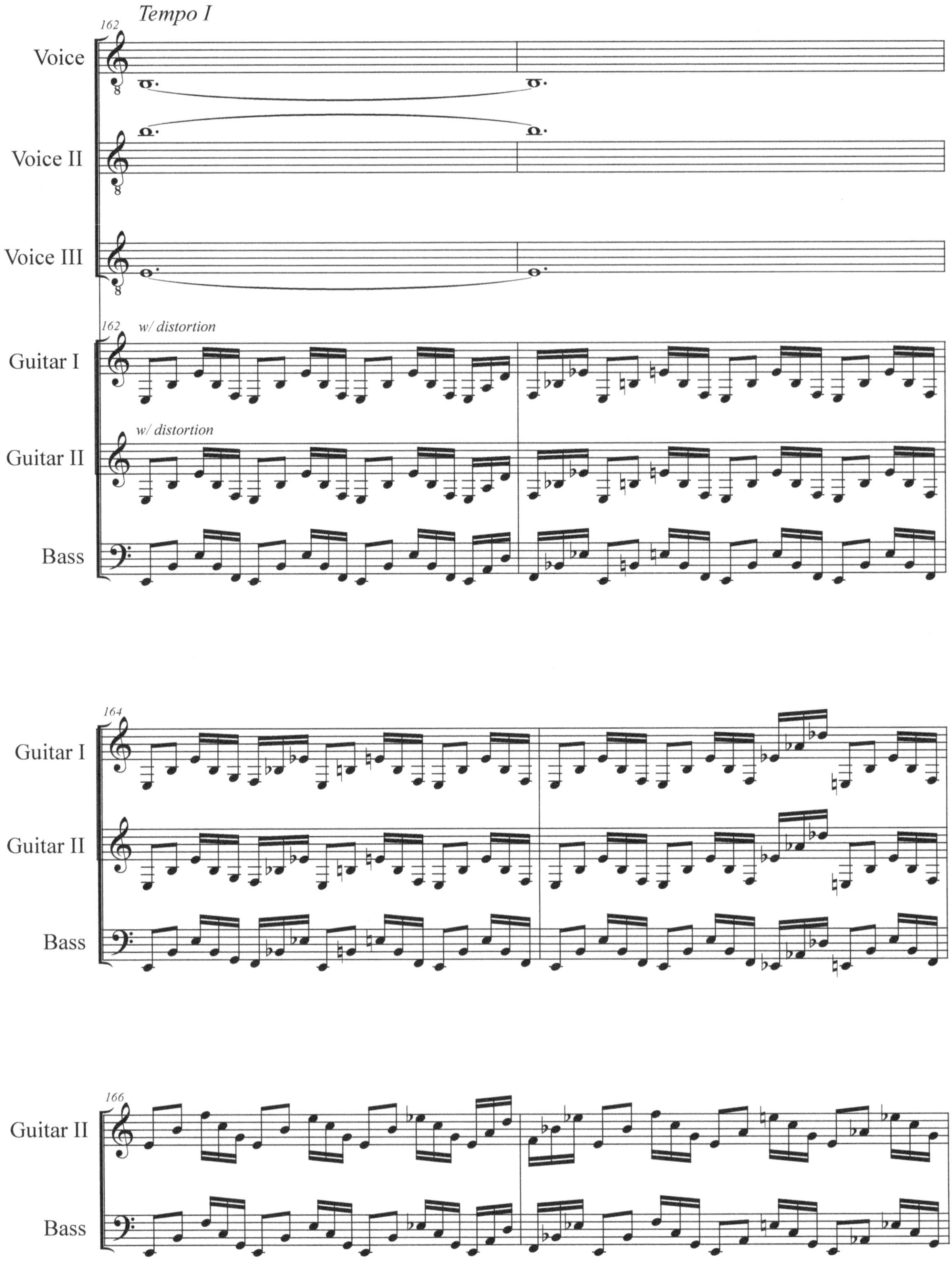
Tempo I
162
Voice
Voice II
Voice III
w/ distortion
Guitar I
w/ distortion
Guitar II
Bass
164
Guitar I
Guitar II
Bass
166
Guitar II
Bass

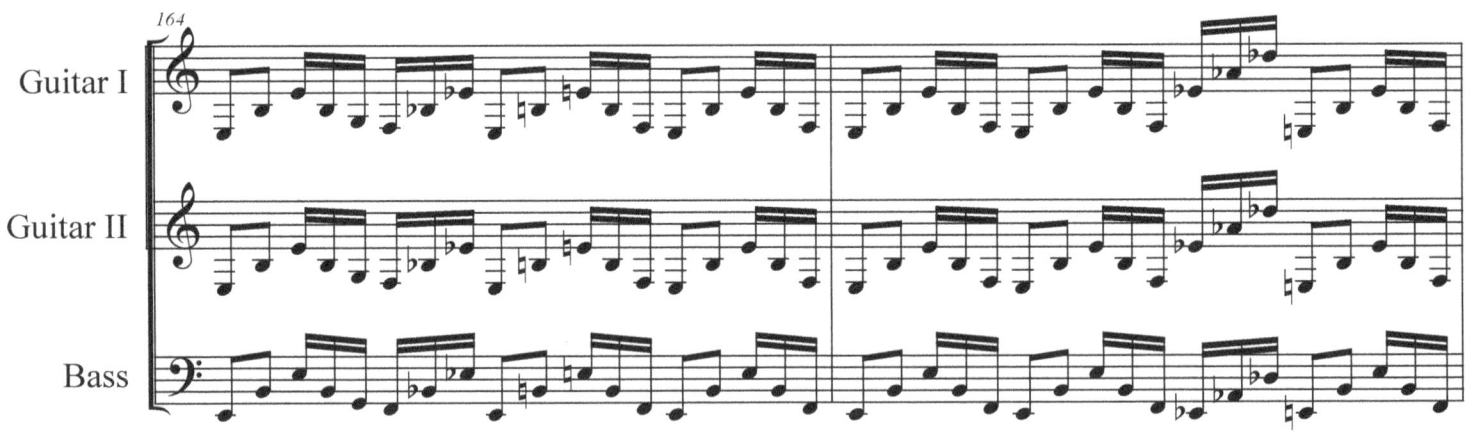

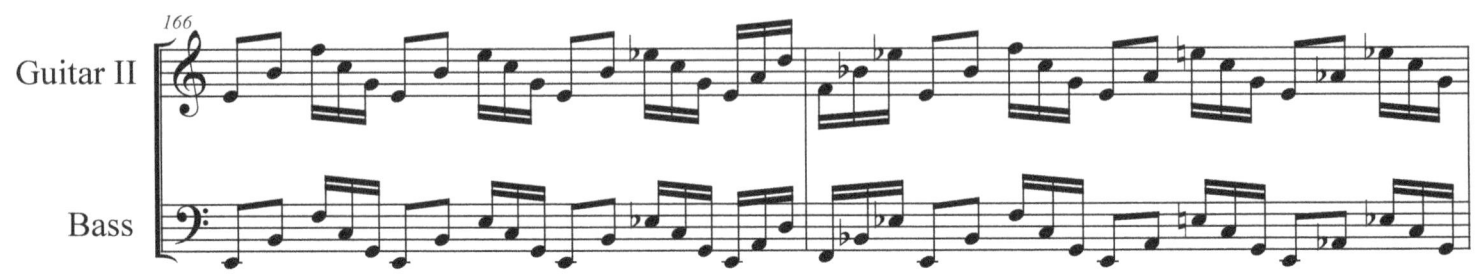

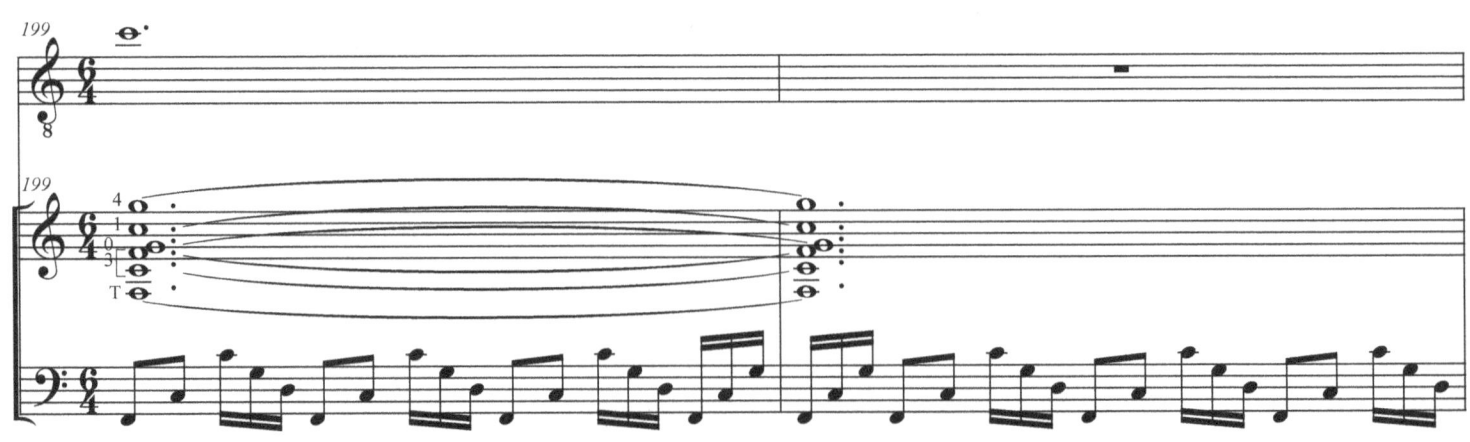

Sleep

Ben Monder

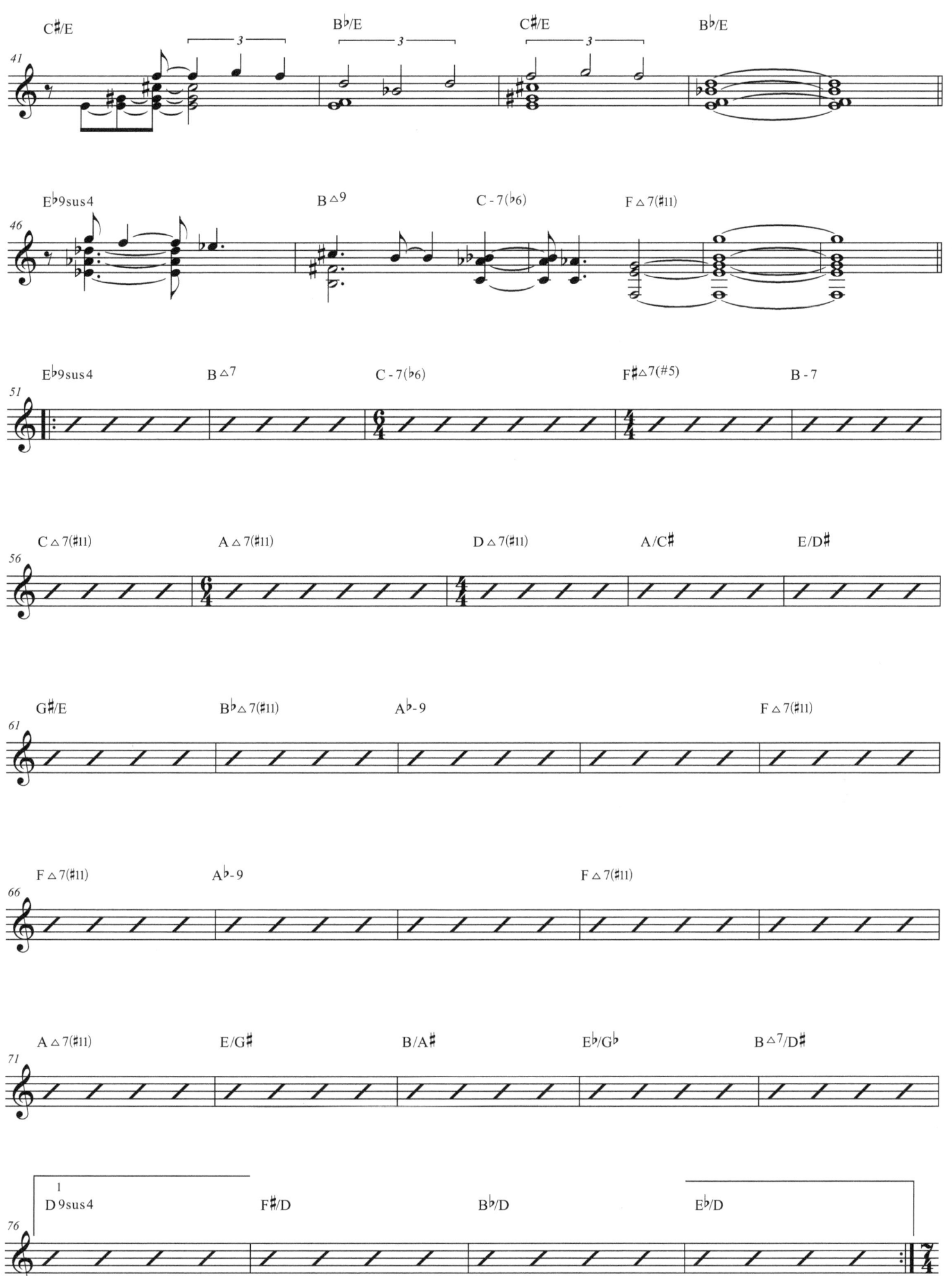

Spectre

Ben Monder

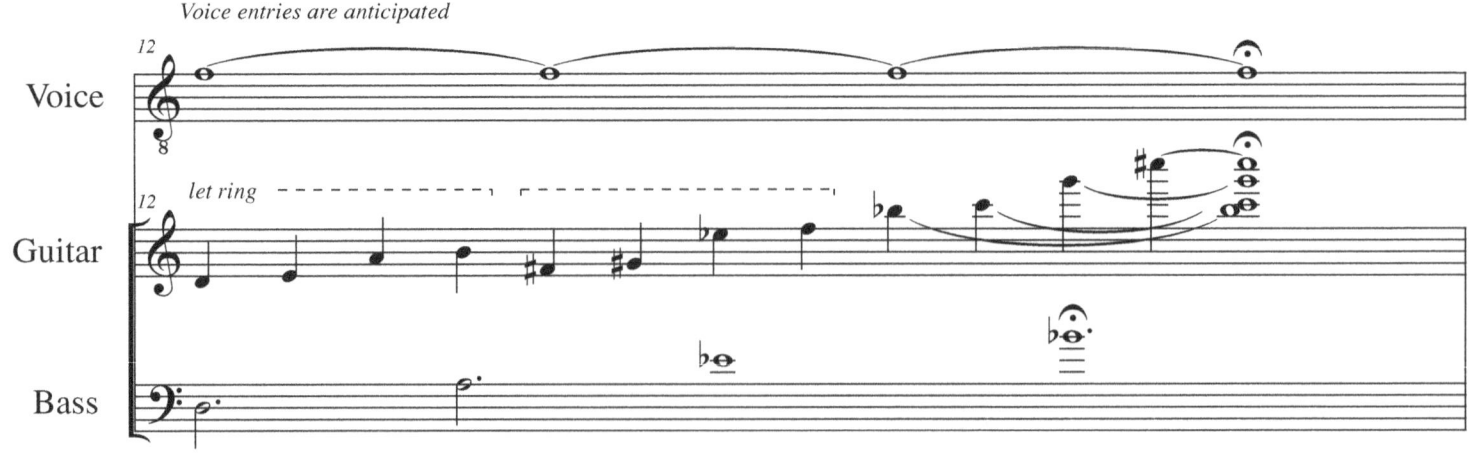
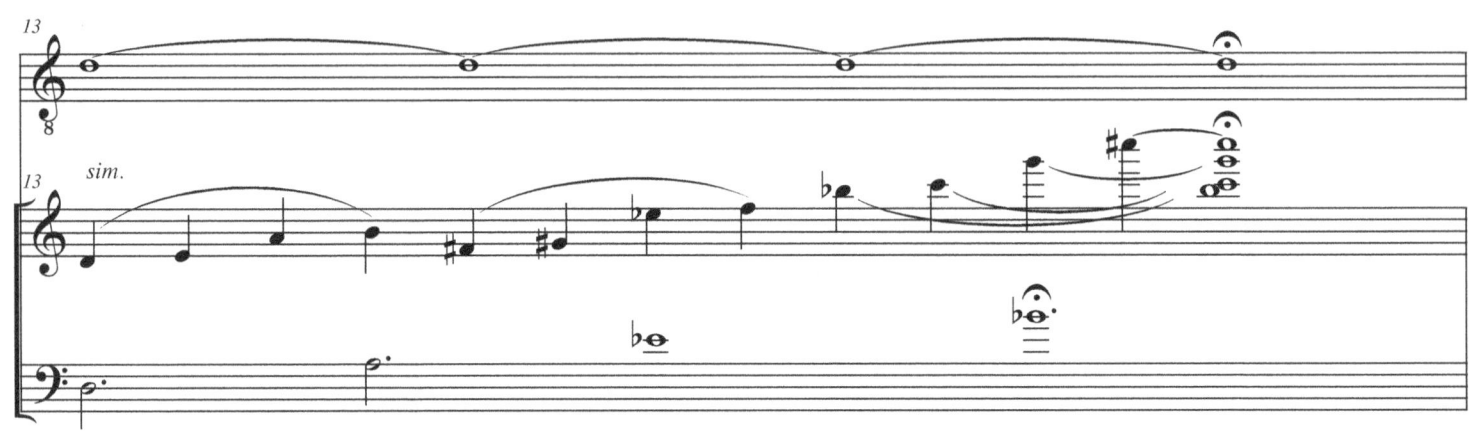
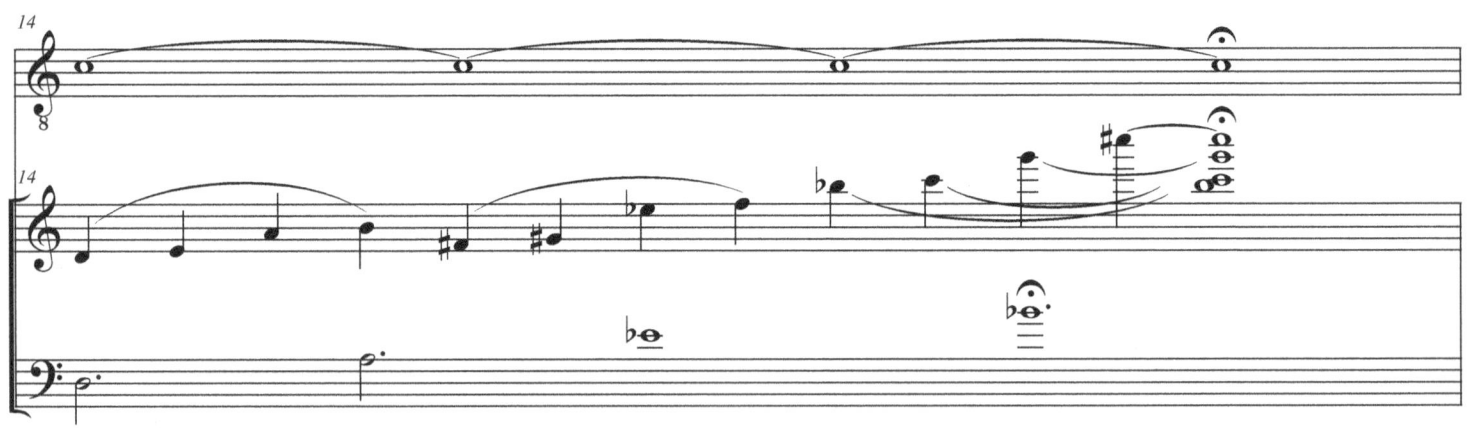
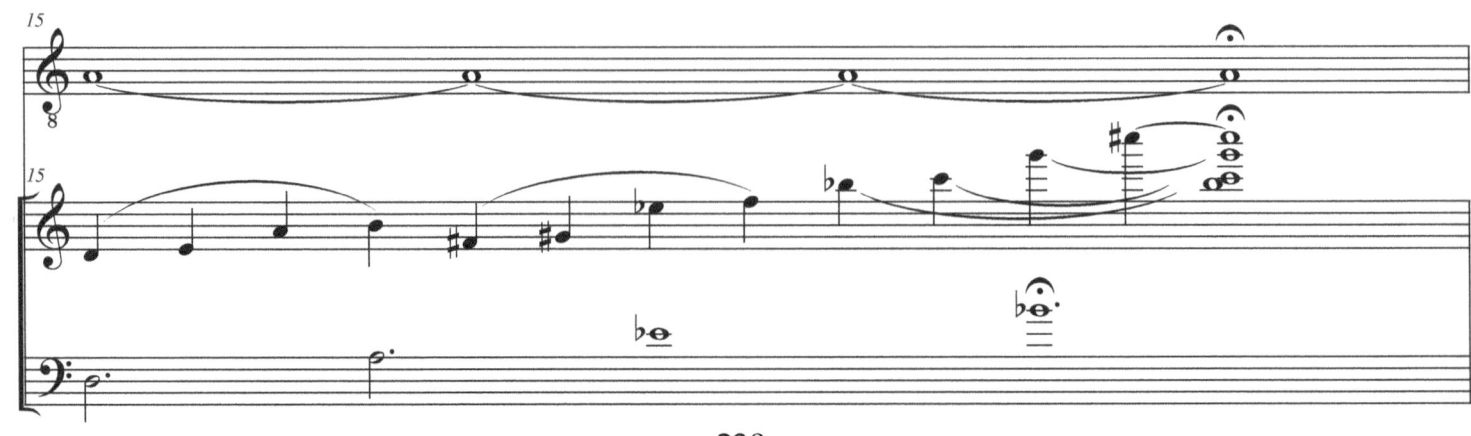

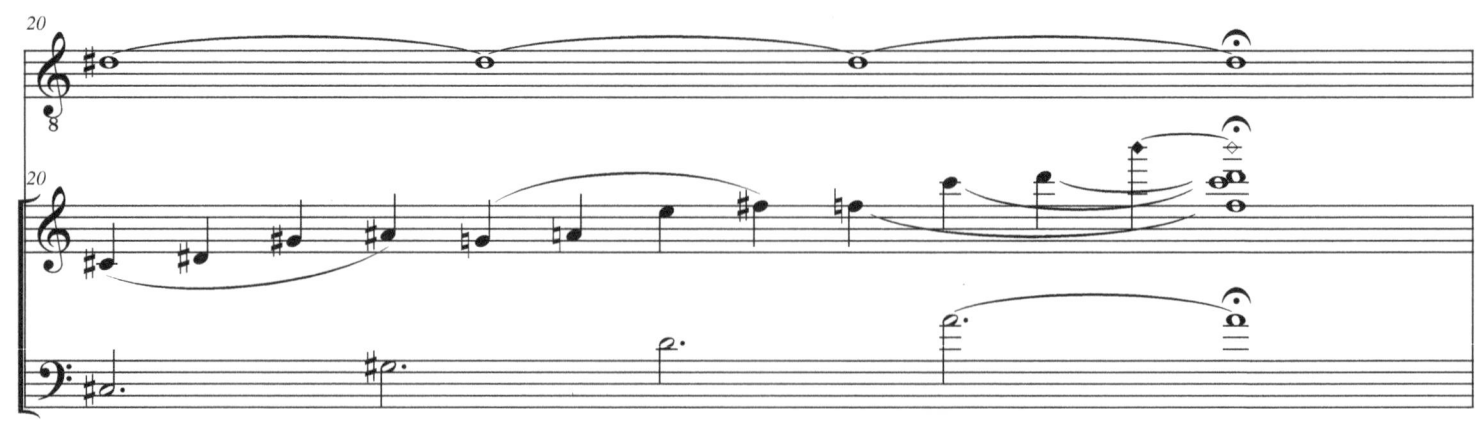

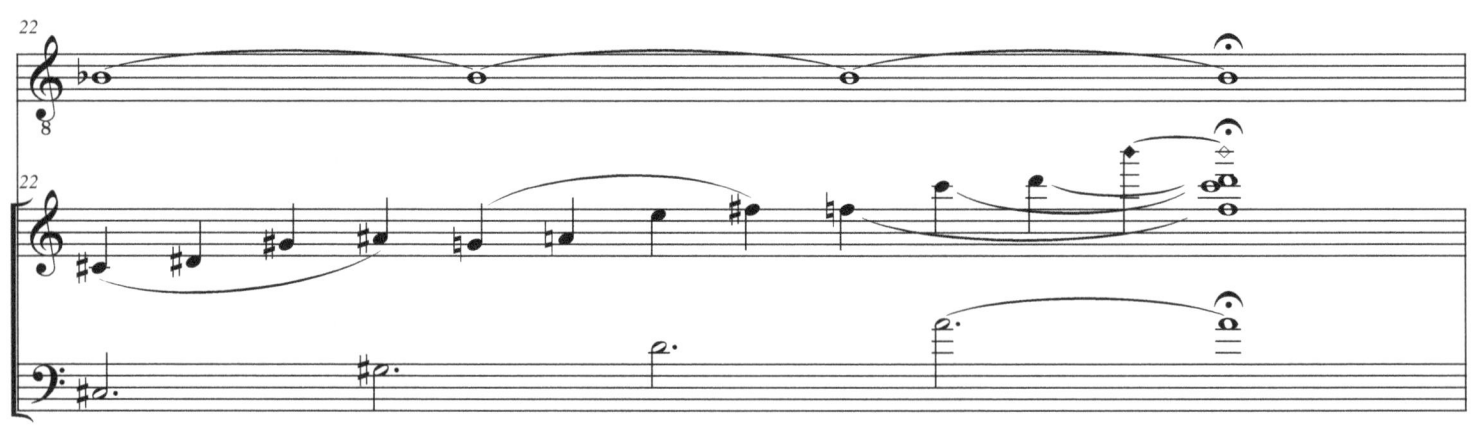
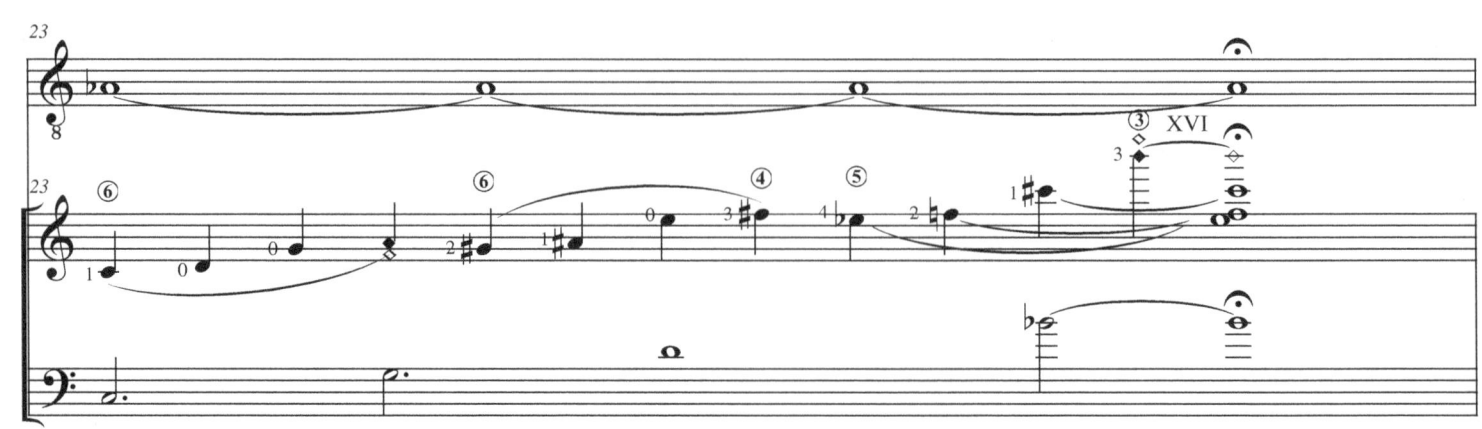

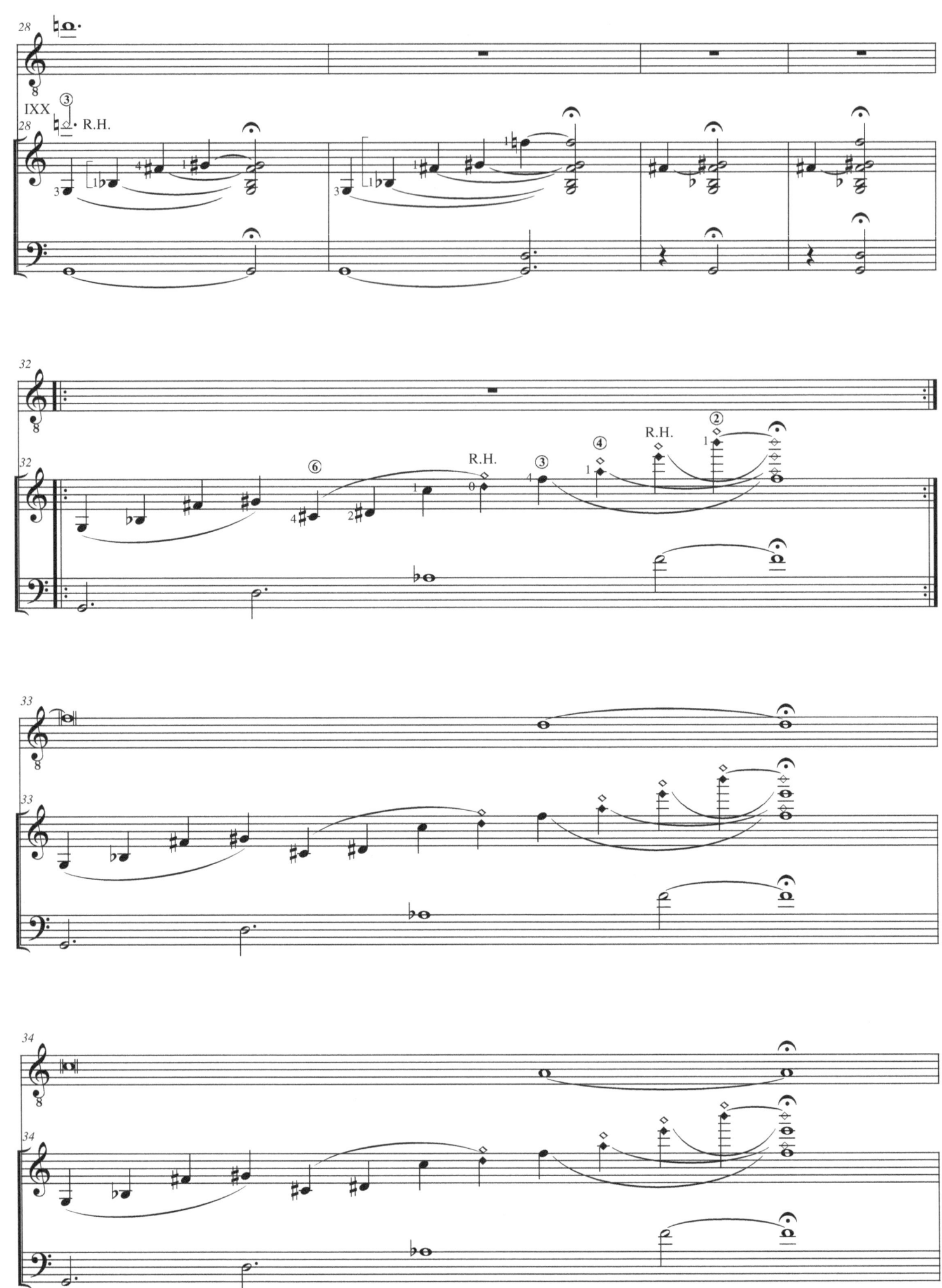

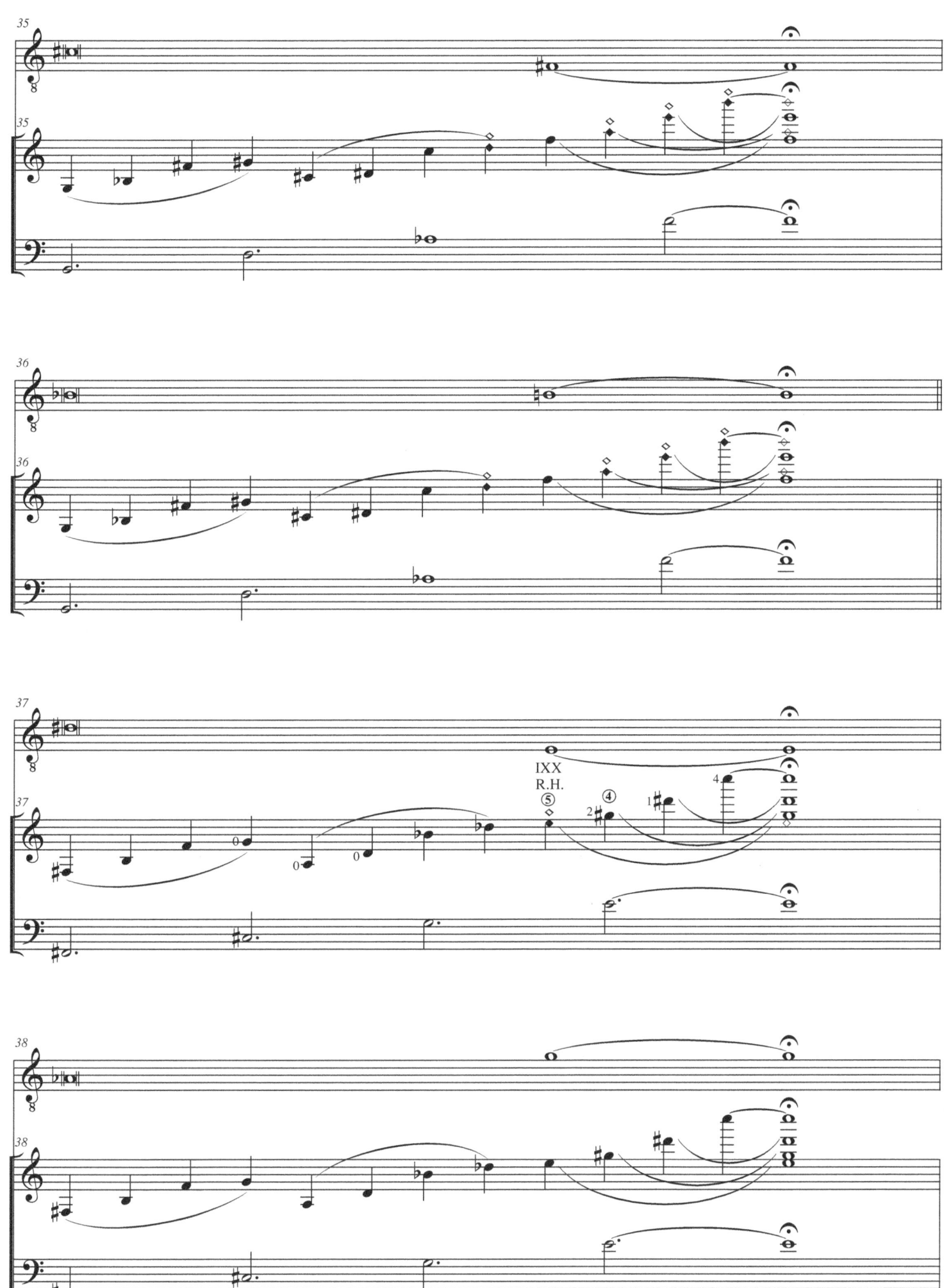

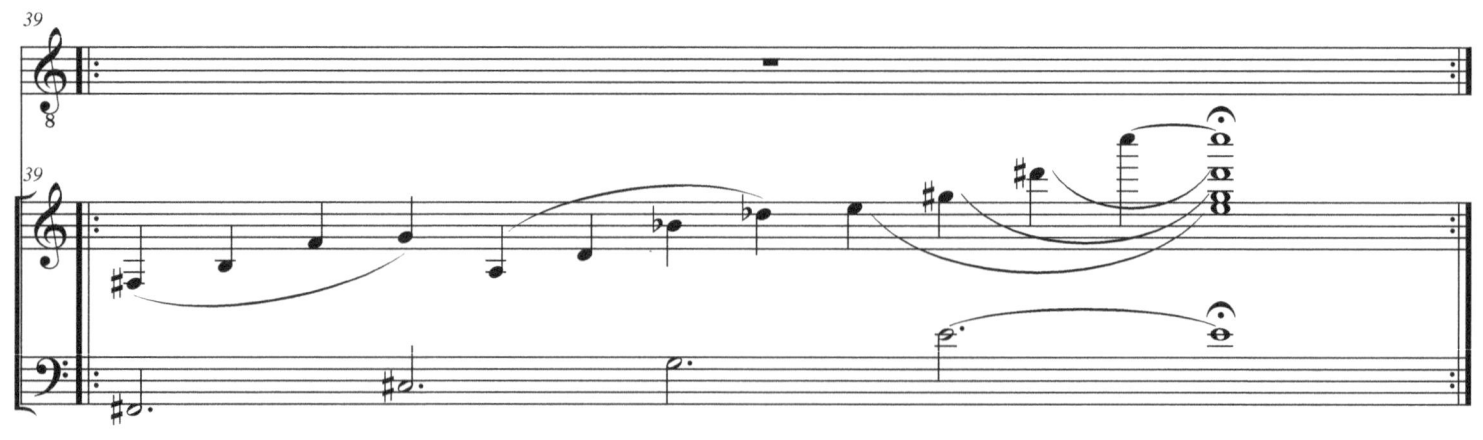
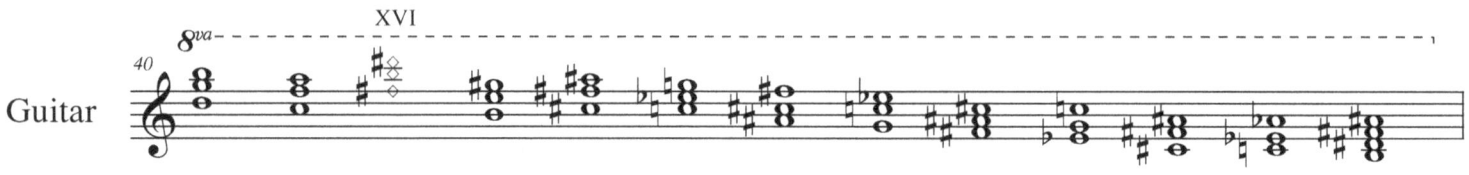

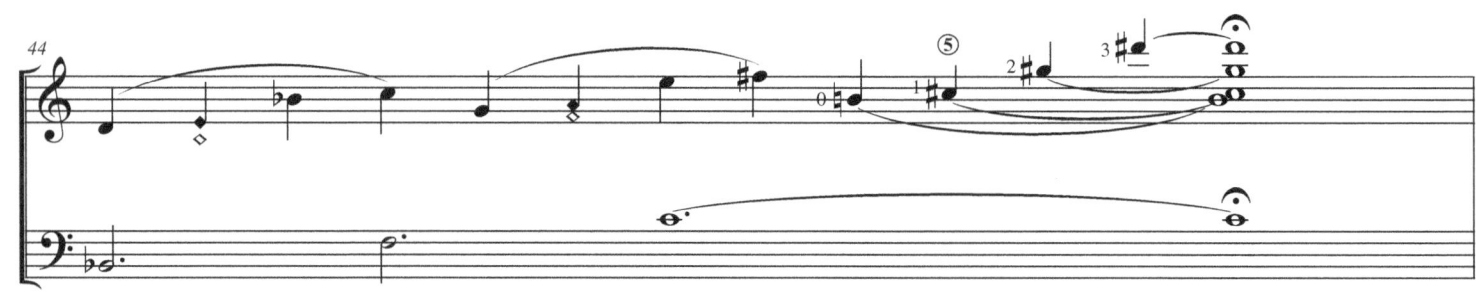

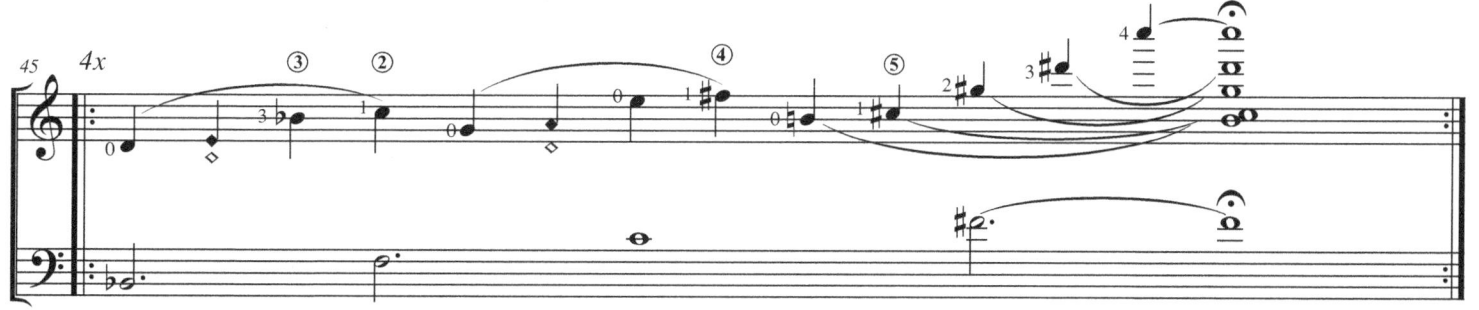
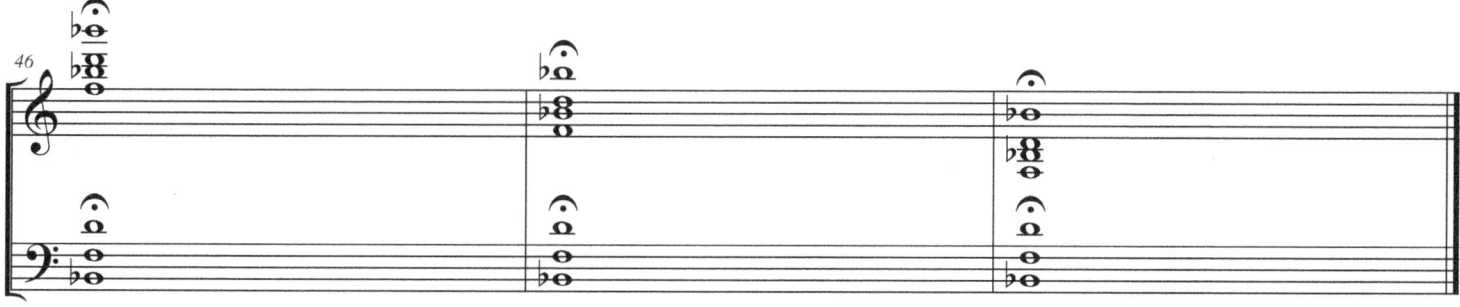

Sunny Manitoba

Ben Monder

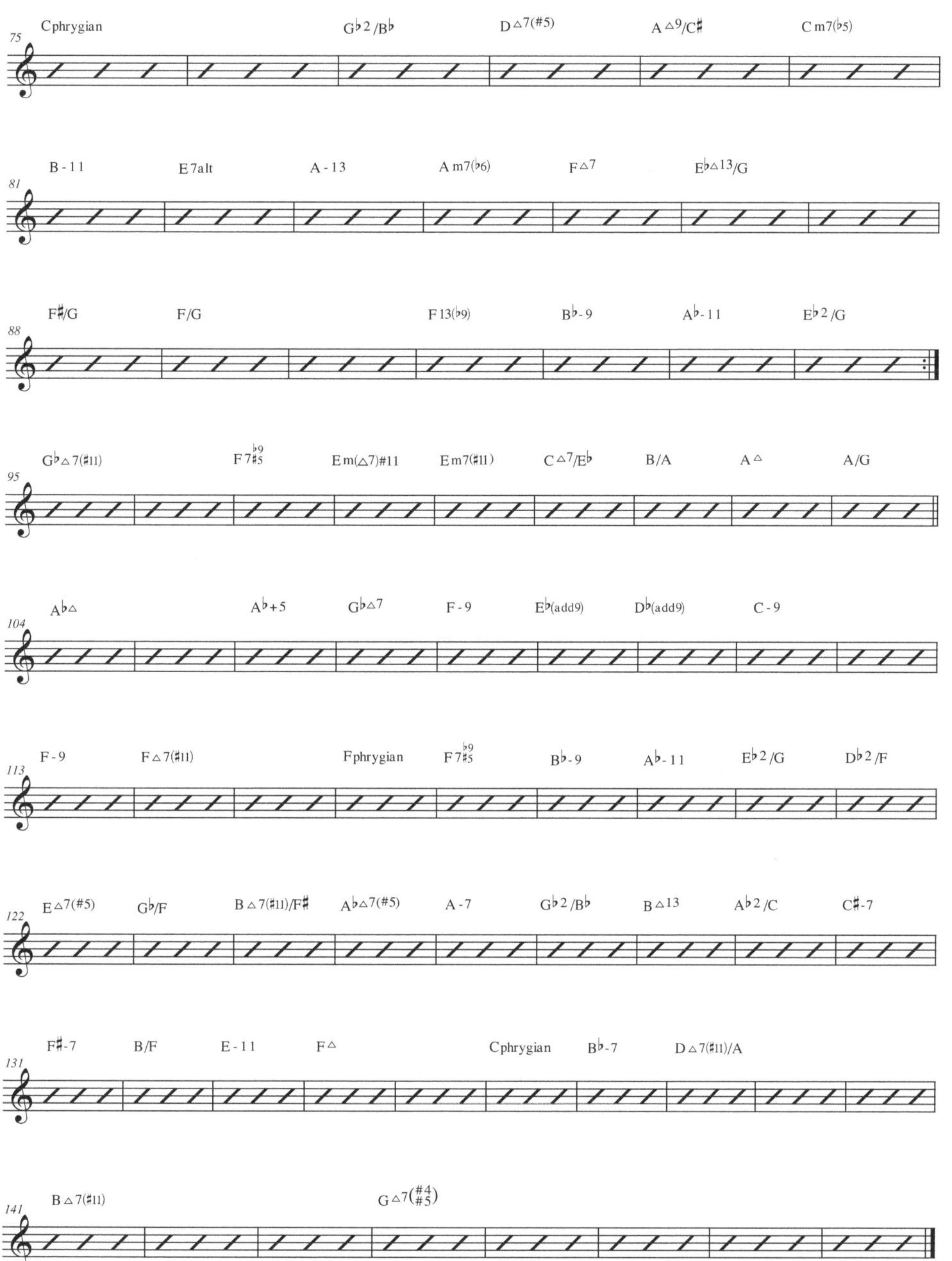

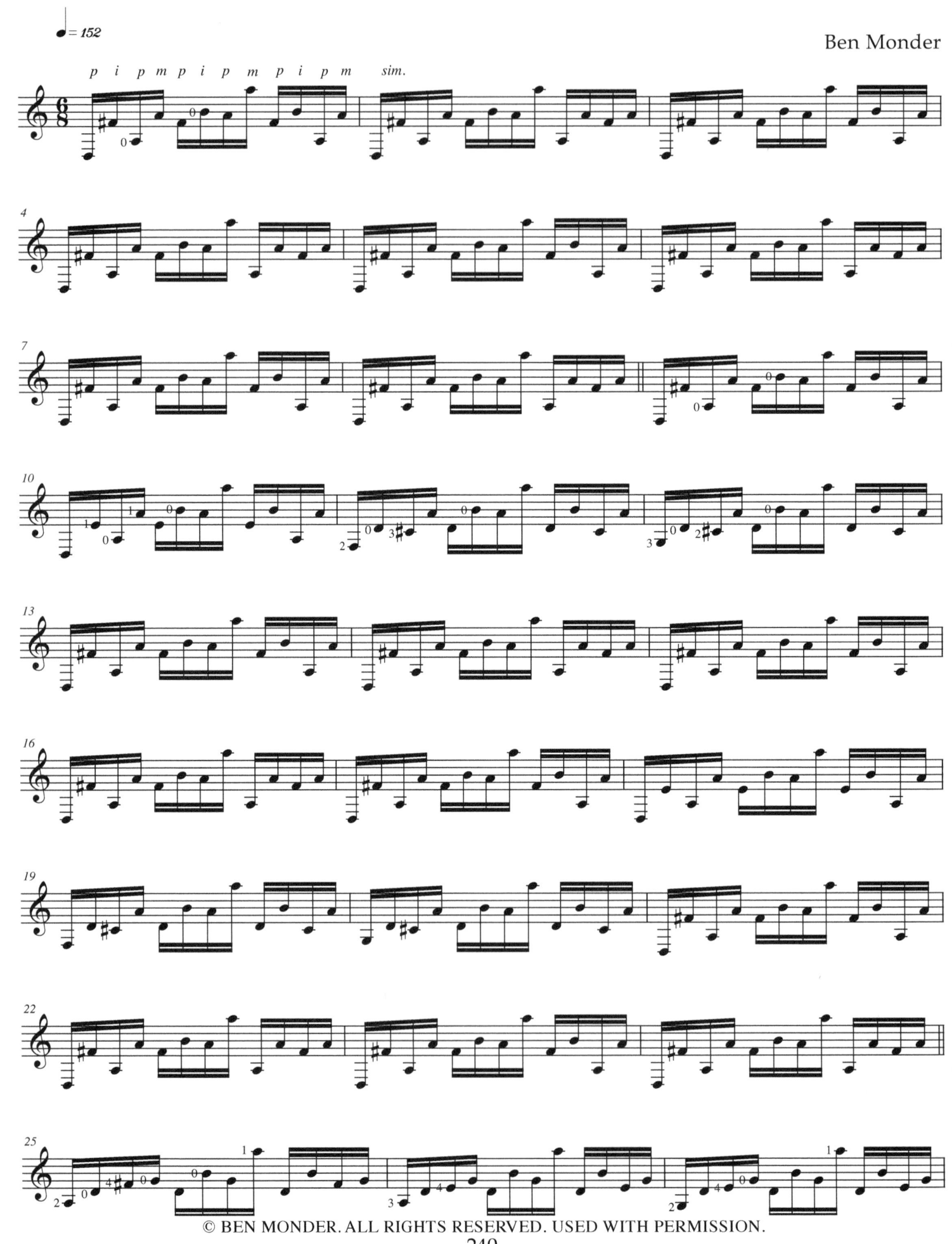

Author's Biography

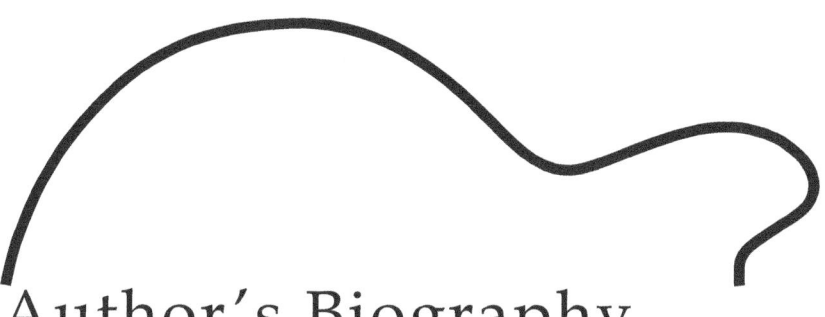

A musician in the New York area for over 20 years, **Ben Monder** has performed with Jack McDuff, Marc Johnson, Lee Konitz, Paul Motian, George Garzone, Kenny Wheeler, and Tim Berne. As a sideman he is busy with a variety of projects, including groups led by Maria Schneider, Paul Motian, Guillermo Klein, Donny McCaslin, Tony Malaby, Bill McHenry, and numerous others. He has conducted clinics and workshops around the world, and has served on the faculty of the New England Conservatory of Music. Ben continues to perform original music internationally with his own quartet, trio, and a duo with vocalist Theo Bleckmann. He has appeared on over 100 CDs as a sideman, and has released 4 as a leader: Oceana (Sunnyside, 2005), Excavation (Arabesque, 2000), Dust (Arabesque, 1997), and Flux (Songlines,1995).